No Regrets

ALSO BY THE AUTHOR:

A Modern Girl's Guide to the Perfect Single Life

A Modern Girl's Guide to Getting Organized

A Modern Girl's Guide to Networking

The Bride's Guide to Unique Weddings

A Modern Girl's Guide to Dynamic Dating: How to Play and Win the Game of Love

A Modern Girl's Guide to Etiquette: How to Get It Right in Every Situation

A Modern Girl's Guide to Getting Hitched

No Regrets

101
Fabulous Things to Do
Before You're
Too Old, Married,
or Pregnant

Sarah Ivens

Illustrations by
Moira Millman

Broadway Books
New York

Published in the United States by Broadway Books, an imprint of The
Doubleday Publishing Group, a division of Random House, Inc., New York.
www.broadwaybooks.com

BROADWAY BOOKS and its logo, a letter B bisected on the diagonal, are
trademarks of Random House, Inc.

Book design by Diane Hobbing of Snap-Haus Graphics

Library of Congress Cataloging-in-Publication Data
Ivens, Sarah.
No regrets : 101 fabulous things to do before you're too old, married,
or pregnant / by Sarah Ivens ; illustrations by Moira Millman. — 1st ed.
p. cm.
1. Women—Life skills guide. I. Title.
HQ1221.I84 2009
646.70082—dc22
2008030414

ISBN 978-0-7679-3031-4

PRINTED IN THE UNITED STATES OF AMERICA

1 3 5 7 9 10 8 6 4 2

First Edition

For Russell

How can I regret anything, when everything
has led me back to you?

Contents

FASHIONISTA SISTA

WILDERNESS WOMAN

JET-SETTER

FREE SPIRIT

CHIC GEEK

CONTENTS

BEAUTY MAVEN

Acknowledgments

To the people who helped me complete this journey: Todd Shuster and Rachel Sussman at Zachary Shuster Harmsworth. You've made it fun! Thanks to Moira Millman, for bringing color to my stories.

To the wonderful women at Broadway Books who saw the relevance of my idea and ran with it: Ann Campbell, Rebecca Cole, Clare Swanson, Hallie Falquet, Ellen Folan, Anne Watters, and the team. I don't regret choosing you!

To my parents, who taught me that life isn't easy but that every hurdle is a chance to learn a lesson: to be stronger, kinder, and braver. Thank you.

To the countless women who contributed to this book. It's fabulous to know I'm in such great company.

Introduction

My thirtieth birthday passed in a whirl of best wishes, drunken dancing, and outrageous merriment. I felt just dandy. There were no soul-searching moments of "oh, damn it, I'm an old hag now" or "where has my life gone?"

Until a few days had passed.

Turning thirty is cool, but being in your thirties can be a bit of a shock. As soon as your helium balloons deflate and your hangover kicks in, you're left asking yourself three things: Is this it? Have I wasted time? Should I have done anything differently? Your experimental years are behind you and suddenly you begin to regret things you haven't done—rather than things you have.

Thankfully I wasn't the only one feeling like this. Friend after friend, cousin after colleague, stared wistfully into their half-empty glasses of pinot grigio at the end of a night out and tortured themselves with men missed and interviews annihilated. Any girl should regret that extra-short dress she wore to a family wedding, the boy she snogged till she was red from stubble rash, or the time she called her best friend a bitch after a few too many tequila slammers in her twenties. Cringe! Yep, maybe we shouldn't have done those things, but we were young and who knew any better?

Regrets for my friends and me are now about opportunities missed and chances not taken. I've been through quite a lot in my life: my parents' divorce, my own divorce, lost friendships, broken hearts, and bad hairdos. But I've managed to learn from all of the above and become a stronger person, with more understanding and kindness toward others and a sense of priority. So those trials aren't what I regret.

What I regret now are the chances not taken. I look back and resent the time I wasted on faux friends, or office gossip, or working for cruel bosses. I regret falling prey to bullies and not making my voice heard.

I don't regret anything I did. I regret what I didn't do. My lack of action. You really need to grab life with both hands—the good times and bad—and say to yourself, "I can handle this."

"The worst moment of my life was sleeping through my university crush climbing up my dorm wall to kiss me good night," laments a good friend and hopeless romantic, Hayley. "My dorm buddies tried to stir me and tell me the good news—yes, he liked me back—but I was half asleep, and instead of throwing on my sneakers and chasing after him, I slept. The next morning I could have killed myself with regret, and he was so mortified by this failed seductive gesture that we never really got together."

"That's nothing," a loudmouth named Jane replied when I told her this story. "I dyed my hair blond for my prom, got hot under the dryer, so sat in my pool to cool down. An hour later I had green hair . . . that was falling out in clumps when I tried to brush it. I wish I'd just spent the money as my friends had and gone to a salon. I missed my prom!"

When we stayed in and missed the party of a lifetime, were we boring? Should we have told the man on the train that we fancied him, seen our inspirational great-aunt more before she died, fought against the in-crowd to stand up for what we believe in? Should we have listened more closely to the words of Lord Jon of Bon Jovi when he sang, "Gonna live while I'm alive/I'll sleep when I'm dead"?

The baggage of regrets weighs a lot and can do your back in. Whether you need to explore new styles, learn to appreciate your loved ones more, or gather the courage to travel the world, I want you to find motivation and encouragement in the following pages. We all have it within us to have wonderful lives. As a wise man once said to me, "The past is finished, the future is unknown, but the present is a gift—open it."

I've talked to and pestered, stalked, and interrogated hundreds of women to find out what we can do to make our waking hours extraordinary and our sleeping hours peaceful. I've dug deep into my own wealth of "bugger thats" and "grrrr" moments to guide you along the path of least regrets. The result is a must-have list of everything wonderful, important, and life affirming that you have to do now . . . before you're too old, married, pregnant, or cynical to be able to change things.

Shoulda, woulda, coulda, schmouda! Don't think about it—do it.

You can't bring the past back for a do-over. So let's try to get it right the first time, and make up your mind to have no regrets.

GLAMOUR GIRL

1 Learn to Love Champagne

Yes, it's expensive, and a nonbeliever might claim it's just another type of sparkling white wine. But open your eyes and see the light, because a cool, crisp flute of champers is the most delicious thing that will ever pass your lips. The delicate flutter of the caramel bubbles across your tongue and the fizzy feeling as they dance down your throat are worth a little extra cash.

Champagne is the most ladylike of beverages. From the first time I tried a taste, I knew there was no way I was going back to the pint glasses of cider and tankards of beer of my student days. Those big, burly drinks suited my university clobber of rugby shirts and baggy jeans, but now, as a professional girl living in London, I deserved a touch of class.

Since that first sip, I've earmarked my most amazing memories with a glass of bubbly. New Year's Eves and weddings are the obvious choices, but champagne is also the perfect way to indulge in more private moments of true happiness. Whenever I arrive on a much-needed vacation, I unpack and explore a little. Then I find the perfect spot (normally somewhere with a vista to take my breath away and ideally where I can run my bare feet through sand) and crack open a bottle. I breathe deeply and feel all my worries melt away.

Or you can simply have a glass during the day (or

evening) with your best friends. The bubbly allows you to be happy that you're together, whether that week is treating you well or not. This is how I discovered that champagne tastes even better with salty french fries. Try it.

Learn to love this old French luxury. Don't drink champagne as though it's going out of fashion—savor each sip. Don't ever drink it warm or out of a plastic glass. And don't ever drink it with people you can't abide—save it for the people you adore and, most of all, for you.

As you're sipping from the flute, think to yourself: I'm lucky. This is the drink of the Golden Age of Hollywood. With a glass of champagne in your hand, you realize the world is a pretty nice place in which to be!

DON'T JUST TAKE IT FROM ME . . .

"My mother and father were always so in love, and I remember watching them get ready for their date nights, which they held once a week. They'd go off to a local restaurant or to dinner and dancing. In preparation for her night out, as she sat at her dressing table applying lotions and potions and brushing her hair, she'd sip a glass of champagne that my father would bring her, perfectly chilled. Champagne to me will always reflect romance and true love."

Barbra, 40, receptionist, Austin

"As I've got older, I've calmed down my drinking a lot. I used to be able to go out and drink wine, then beer, then shots . . . The day I turned thirty, I decided that my head—and waistline—couldn't take it anymore. So now I believe in quality, not quantity. And I feel much more refreshed and spoiled having three glasses of champagne on a night out than two bottles of mediocre wine. And my hangovers are not so nearly as painful!"

Lucy, 32, writer, Brooklyn

IF YOU CAN'T LEARN TO LOVE CHAMPAGNE . . .

Get your own signature drink that makes you feel decadent and fabulous. Find something that suits you—a drink that allows you to have fun without falling over. It should be a festive cocktail that people know to order for you as soon as you walk through the door. If you have a favorite fruit, find a tipple that is flavored with it and your favorite spirit. Heck, find a friendly barman and get him to invent a drink in your honor! If you're not a drinker, explore delicious smoothies or flavored teas for a special treat.

2 Eat French Fries—Without a Side of Guilt

In this weight-obsessed world, it's too easy to dismiss the culinary pleasures of our childhood: chocolate milk shakes, Jell-O, gummi bears . . . and french fries! Life is too short to avoid these delicious strands of potato. You can be a skinny mini anytime, but finding the perfect fry, or "chip" as we call them in England, is a pleasure too good to pass up.

The most divine fry I've ever tasted was in the

Cayman Islands. I'd booked the trip to de-stress and to get away from a rainy January in New York (scientists have decided that the third Monday of January is officially the most depressing day of the year, and this trip was all that got me through it!). As soon as I got to the island, I heard the locals and fellow tourists alike raving about the parmesan-encrusted, truffle-oil-cooked french fries offered at the Periwinkle diner in my hotel. I knew they would make my vacation all the more special, so I headed to Periwinkle. The golden batons arrived, and with every bite I thrilled a little more and made my way to the pearly gates of carbohydrate heaven. Crispy on the outside, yet deliciously soft in the middle. With ketchup, without ketchup. With a swig of rum punch or a sip of water, they were friggin' scrumptious, to use an English phrase.

You don't have to be in a five-star hotel in the Caribbean to enjoy the french fry, though—they taste just as good in a greasy diner with a hangover or with your godchildren at a hamburger joint. Yes, we have to be sensible and healthy, but a little bit of what you fancy does you good.

DON'T JUST TAKE IT FROM ME . . .

"French fries remind me of my growing up with my four brothers and sisters. Every summer we'd head to my grandparents' in South Carolina for four weeks. On Sundays, Grandpa would take us to Myrtle Beach to walk the boardwalk and play the arcade games. We'd ride the roller coaster, then, still feeling slightly dizzy and nauseous, we'd head over to the food stall and eat fries until we recovered."

Jill, 28, waitress, Charlotte, North Carolina

"The one thing I was told about your wedding day is that it would fly by too quickly—and how right they were! Mine whizzed past in a flash, in a whirl of friends, family, photos, toasts, gifts . . . all lovely stuff, but I forgot to eat. Oh, and talk to my new husband! Thank God for room service. At two in the morning we headed up to our room, ordered a club sandwich and fries, and gossiped and laughed about all the memories we'd just made downstairs with all our loved ones. That is still my most romantic meal ever."

Sarah, 33, writer, Brooklyn

IF YOU CAN'T HELP FEELING GUILTY FOR EATING FRENCH FRIES . . .

Shame on you! Look, we all have to think about our waistlines and keep our hearts healthy, but we all need to have fun, too. If you can't totally indulge in anything fried, why not look for french fries cooked without trans fats or find some that are oven baked. Also, try sweet-potato fries—they have a much higher nutritional value than fries made from plain potatoes.

3 Rock the Microphone at Karaoke

Too often, we're ruled by fear. It stops us from doing things that would really be rather fun if only we had the guts to try them. Nothing is as fun—or frightening— as singing in front of others, especially if you've got a voice like a cat being strangled. But if everyone's eardrums can stand it, what's to fear? At the very worst, you'll make people laugh and reach for the cocktail list—and there's no harm in that!

I was lucky (or unlucky) to grow up in a karaoke family. Lacking that embarrassment gene, my two brothers and I would happily torture my parents for hours on end. Then my parents caught the bug. Now every New Year's Eve is party time at the Ivenses' house.

As soon as people get "on stage," they don't want to leave that bit of carpet in the middle of the living room. The clapping, cheering, yelps of encouragement, and moment in the spotlight are all too enthralling to give up. Sometimes we've had to physically wrestle the microphone off some overzealous chanteuse.

The thing to remember about karaoke is it's only a bit of fun—no one expects you to be Tina Turner and belt out an amazing tune. It's all about being silly, having a moment of glory, making your friends laugh, and letting out your inner rock god. Don't let all this pass you by because you have a less-than-perfect voice—just find a song to suit you.

I have found that mimicking a song by a female pop star is the way forward. Madonna, Janet Jackson, and Debbie Gibson—their songs are reasonably easy to croon along to. Or pick a classic that everyone will join in with, camouflaging your mangled tones. The best ones for this route are "American Pie" by Don McLean, "Summer of '69" by Bryan Adams, or anything by Guns N' Roses. The other option for the vocally impaired is to go down rap alley. A colleague of mine does an impressive crowd-swelling version of

Young MC's "Bust a Move" (and she won't mind my saying she can't sing a note!).

Other good options include "White Lines" by Grandmaster Flash, Melle Mel, and the Furious 5 and "Ice Ice Baby" by Vanilla Ice. Everyone will be so impressed that you are keeping up with the lyrics, no one will care what you sound like. So start thinking about what your signature song can be and get practicing.

DON'T JUST TAKE IT FROM ME . . .

"There is a fabulous dive bar in New York's Chinatown that starts up the karaoke machine at midnight. You can order in take-out noodles from the restaurant next door, and everyone who sings gets a free shot. Each time me and my friends go, it's the same . . . we argue about who's going to get up first. Then we do our favorite tune (Phil Collins's "Easy Lover") and we're hooked. It's great—we can control the music!"

Enid, 24, student, Trenton, New Jersey

"After I split up with my husband a few years ago, I was down in the dumps and found it hard to have fun. But my friends were fabulous and made me go out with them. The safest, nearest place to my private sanctuary (my apartment) was a karaoke bar. One song soon became my anthem—"I Will Survive"! I sang it terribly, but because the sentiment there was so strong—especially after a few mojitos—everyone cheered me on and I sang it with feeling. Now I screech that song out wherever I am and it reminds me how far I've come."

Janice, 39, receptionist, Dunwoody, Georgia

Learn a dance routine. Your audience will be so distracted by your impressive grapevine-clap-twirl combo that they won't even notice your bum notes. Or get a singing partner who is so impressive that you can just relax and do backing vocals, earning a big round of applause anyway.

4 Let an Unsuitable Man Spoil You Rotten

Every woman deserves to be swept away on the sea of romance at least once in her life. Yes, it should be only a temporary loss of good sense and judgment, but hooking up with a boy toy, a sugar daddy, or a Casanova can feel naughty but nice.

A boy toy is great for fun and making you feel young again—he won't have the same issues and worries as men your age. Let's face it, relationships tend to turn us from confident, happy people into insecure, nervous wrecks—but if you get one young enough (but over the age of eighteen, please), he won't have had nightmare girlfriends to warp him yet. Oh, and perhaps best of all, a boy toy can update your iPod for you.

Sugar daddies are so good for moments of indulgence because it's a mutually beneficial relationship you're creating: the old boys are happy to be seen out with a gorgeous young thang, and you like to be treated like a lady (a skill that unfortunately too many young men have forgotten).

Casanovas love the ladies. It started with their mothers and sisters, and now it goes down the chain to every woman they pass in the street. They love big boobs, small boobs, long hair, short hair, red lips, glossy pouts, a girlish laugh, and an icy stare—and they make you feel like a million dollars. The problem is, they make every other woman feel like a million dollars, too. As long as you realize that and either (a) don't expect a serious relationship, or (b) lobotomize your jealous streak and live with their flirtatious ways, you'll be fine.

Date one of these fun types for the excitement. But call game over before you end up dysfunctional and alone. Just one encounter should be enough to make you realize that when it comes to long-term happiness, there is nothing wrong with the kind man you've met who makes you laugh. You don't need a stereotype—just a really nice chap.

DON'T JUST TAKE IT FROM ME . . .

"I felt like a dirty old woman when I first started seeing Fergus, the sexy barman from my local hangout. He was twenty-one and I'm ashamed to say I was thirty-one. But he made me laugh and I made him smile, and we had the most rocking time. We didn't share the same taste in music, films, or books, but that helped us keep independent and interesting to the other one."

Jenevora, 41, travel planner, Southampton, England

"I met a man twenty-five years older than me and I was flattered by his attention. I didn't feel as nervous stripping in front of him as I would have been with a guy my own age, so our love life was much more exciting than you'd imagine. He felt grateful to be with me, and although this wouldn't have been a healthy balance long term, my sugar daddy got me through a tough period in my life."

Wendy, 30, marketing manager, Los Angeles

IF YOU CAN'T LET AN UNSUITABLE MAN SPOIL YOU ROTTEN . . .

Keep whatever relationship you are in romantic. Spoil each other. Make sure you talk to your partner about more than just work, bills, and housework. This sounds simple, but it's easy to get tied down with the minutia of modern living and forget to have fun. Go to the cinema to watch cheesy comedies. Play your favorite albums from your teenage years while you're cleaning the house. Forget about your diets and head to a burger bar for a pig-out. Ask each other mind-expanding questions with answers that keep you surprised: who would play you in a film, which book do you wish you'd written, what is your fondest childhood memory, and so on.

5 Throw Yourself a Party

Why should a fabulous person like you have to wait for someone else to plan a party for you? First of all, surprise parties are overrated. Some loose-lipped buddy always slips up and gives away the surprise. And when someone offers to throw you a party, it's very kind, but then you worry whether she's invited the right people and planned an evening that reflects the real you (and you can't express any of these worries, because she's being sweet to do it). You can avoid a lot of hassle if you send out your own invites and plan your own event.

Do you need a reason to throw a party? Hell no! I've found these reasons to be equally appealing to guests:

> It's January, it's cold, and we need
>> something to cheer us up.
> It's July, it's summer, and I need to
>> make the most of my roof deck.
> I've got a new house, and I need you lot
>> to help me destroy the carpet.
> It's Oscar night, so let's all laugh at the
>> dresses together.
> It's Super Bowl Sunday, and the calories
>> in pizza and wings don't count if we
>> eat them in front of one another and
>> the television.
> And of course, the classic: it's my
>> birthday, I'm getting older, and you
>> need to help me drink to forget.

Last year I was feeling particularly in need of celebration. I was spending my first birthday in ten years as a singleton—and to rub it in, one of my younger brothers and his wife had just had an adorable baby boy. I was moving backward while everyone around me was moving forward, and my birthday was a massive reminder of that.

Donna, a dear childhood friend of mine, had just been through a nasty broken engagement and needed something fabulous to look forward to as well. With our birthdays three days apart, it was obvious what we should do: have a party.

I asked an artist friend to design stylish invitations, which we sent to 150 of the most fabulous, beloved people in our lives. Then, on a balmy Friday evening, on the roof of Soho House overlooking the bustling streets of London, we celebrated getting older. And being single. And our love of margaritas. We partied from 6 p.m. to 3 a.m. and everyone had an amazing time (despite having only one CD—thankfully it was a Whitney!).

You don't need to have a huge bash. People love a party of any size. It's an excuse to get tipsy, dance to music you'd never hear played in a trendy nightclub, get free drinks, and socialize with lots of people you already know and like. How fabulous.

After throwing more than fifty parties in my time, I can share a magic secret: it's all about the music and people. Make sure both of these are fun, cool, and energetic, and everything else is icing on the cake. Allow for five cocktails or glasses of wine per person (nothing kills an event like a dry bar). And if you're going posh and serving hors d'oeuvres, allow seven per person—and a snack at midnight always goes down a treat (think bacon sandwiches, bagels, or even baskets of marshmallows and cups of hot chocolate if you're sending people home). Cheap thrills at parties include organizing midnight dance-offs or hula-hoop competitions and offering up cheap and cheerful goody bags of sweets and balloons as people exit.

So go on, become the hostess with the mostess at least once in your life. It'll instantly increase your fabulousity. There are not many buzzes like the one you get when the best people in your life are all together and having fun because of you.

DON'T JUST TAKE IT FROM ME . . .

"I'm quite a homebody—I've never been a club person or a barhopper. So a few years ago I learned that the best way to handle this and remain social was to turn my home into party central. And I love it . . . Any excuse, and I'll throw open my doors and start pouring the punch. If Oprah has a landmark show on, it's a girls' night. If the Mets are playing the Yankees, it's a beer and nachos bash. I bought a wide-screen television and a huge fridge, and now my place is the hottest venue in town."
Clara, 32, marketing manager, New York City

"Throwing parties was always my thing. My friends think I'm quite bossy—but in a good way that means I get people organized into having a good time. I took this to an extreme last year, when my husband and I moved into a big, old Victorian house with a shed. We converted the shed into a pub, complete with a jukebox, slot machines, a full bar, and a mirror ball on the ceiling. I like being queen bee, of course, but the one problem is, we've made it so fab, I never get invited out anymore. Everyone comes to us!"
Kathleen, 30, bar manager, Louisville, Kentucky

IF YOU CAN'T THROW YOURSELF A PARTY . . .

Even if you haven't got the financial means to throw a party, you can still become social secretary for your

group of friends. Everyone needs a little encouragement—especially in the winter when it's miserable
outside. Suggest a big night out with your girls.
Organize a guest list at a new club, or find out who has
a ladies' night where drinks are free (or two for one, at
least). Read the local paper to find out what's just
opened or been revamped, when your favorite bands
are in town, or what free events—such as outdoor
movie nights—are happening soon, and then invite
your best pals to join you.

6 Get Thrown Out of a Nightclub

Now, I'm not the kind of girl to condone antisocial behavior, and despite being a Brit, I am in no way your
typical English hooligan. I have never endorsed kicking strangers, vomiting in public, or gesturing with
abandon at passersby. I do, however, totally recommend getting thrown out of a nightclub just once in
your life.

A fabulous nightclub is a wonderful thing. From
Les Caves du Roy in Saint-Tropez (the home of the
most expensive bottle of champagne I've been foolish
enough to purchase) to Tao in Las Vegas (a favorite of
Britney's, but we won't hold that against it), nothing
can bond you and a gaggle of your best girls like a
night out underneath a gigantic glitter ball.

The anticipation of an evening doing something
more than going to the cinema or heading out for a
meal is intoxicating. It's not just about getting to the

nightclub and shaking your tush to the latest tunes. No, no, it's all about the anticipation. It's the hours spent getting ready—the Saturday trawl of the mall for the perfect outfit, the preparation in front of the mirror (think *try on, twirl, repeat*), highlighting your face with the perfect smoky eye and bronzed cheek combo, and spraying your wrists with your sexiest scent. This, followed by a confidence-boosting margarita and a spin around your living room to Christina Aguilera, and you're just about ready to rock.

Once you and your posse have strutted into the venue, turning every male head in the place, it's time to misbehave. There's nothing worse than just sitting down wistfully or propping up the bar, waiting to be chatted up by your dream man. However much of an inner Bridget Jones you have burning inside you, silence her by having wild, unadulterated fun.

Jump into the DJ booth and give a big shout-out to your friends, set the club alight with a round of Flaming Drambuies, or even work out a dance routine beforehand and take over the dance floor en masse when "Thriller" comes on. I've done this, and it's fabulous. Rather than waiting like a wallflower for a man to buy you a drink, buy your own and have fun fun fun till the lights come up—or a security guard removes you from the dance floor and shows you the door.

I've been chucked out of a nightclub twice, but to be honest, once would have been enough. The first time I was dismissed for trying to get my fellow party people to stage a sit-down protest because the DJ wouldn't play Tiffany's "I Think We're Alone Now." The second time was for pouring an electric blue cocktail over a man (a.k.a. a pair of hands) for being a disgusting pervert. I argued that *he* should have been given his marching orders, not me, but he was a regular and a banker—two things in his favor, which left him free to move on to another unsuspecting bottom.

Both dismissals were humiliating for, oh, fifteen seconds, and then my "no regrets" mind-set kicked in and I found each situation amusing.

The main reason you won't regret getting chucked out? It's the easiest way to prove to your children, grandchildren, or lover that you were not always the picture of sense and sobriety! That you indeed were once so rebellious and crazy that people made the effort to remove you from their den of sin.

It's a laugh to get tossed, and life offers too few of those. As long as you've got some money to get home and your friends know where you are (hand signal to them as you're being dragged away), enjoy it.

NB: Let me just quickly add that all throwing-out should occur at a decently young age—mutton dressed as lamb being shown the door is not so much rebellious as tragic. Do it while you're young. And don't make a habit of it—I warn you against getting chucked out of nightclubs becoming a monthly thing. No one likes a drunk or an inmate.

DON'T JUST TAKE IT FROM ME . . .

"I'm proud to say I've been chucked from a nightclub where I thought anything goes and all kind of bad behavior is accepted—Culture Club in New York City. On one occasion, after downing a few too many Ronald Reagan shots, my friend and I got overexcited to hear "Mickey" by Toni Basil and we decided to throw ourselves on the backs of some passing men. They dropped us—sprawling—to the floor. So I jumped on my friend's back, she wobbled on her high heels, and we both dropped to the floor again, tipsy and hysterical. Even the security team pulling us to our feet and wrestling us toward the exit couldn't stop us from peeing ourselves with laughter. The next day we had bruises from resisting arrest, but the bruises faded within days. The giggle-inducing flashbacks have lasted years and years."

Andrea, 31, music producer, Los Angeles

"When my marriage ended and I was spending my days licking my wounds, eventually my friends said enough was enough—they took me shopping and then took me dancing. I realized what I'd been missing during my twenties—the chance to let loose, get tipsy, and flirt, all while doing the electric slide! Yes, I got chucked out once (for erotic dancing on a pole, if you can believe it), but don't miss out on this chance for fun."

Sara, 32, editor, New York City

IF YOU CAN'T GET THROWN OUT OF A NIGHTCLUB . . .

Make out with the DJ. Even if he hasn't been tickled with the handsome brush, he's cool because he's the DJ. If you don't want to be naughty in public, throw your own bash that can be as wild as you like (without ruining the carpets). Strictly speaking, you can't get thrown out of your own party, but you can get so outrageously drunk and disorderly that your boyfriend or best friend throws you out of the melee and into your pajamas, then into bed.

7 Eat in a Fancy Restaurant by Yourself

Care too much about what others think? Uh-huh! We all do. We're all so self-aware that we get paranoid about what other people think about us.

This stops us from living as freely and pleasurably, or even as practically, as we should.

Even successful, independent women can feel that going out to restaurants alone makes them look like lonely losers. This notion promotes far too many nights sucked into the television with a nasty microwave meal on our laps or an extortionately priced room-service dinner eaten alone in a hotel room while traveling.

Why do we feel like this? Do you have a niggling feeling that if you ventured into a restaurant to dine alone, the room would stop and stare? The clatter of cutlery would halt as couples whispered in your direction and waiters—thinking that to eat alone you surely must be a few sandwiches short of a picnic—would hover in case you did a runner without paying the check?

I hate to break it to you, sunshine, but you're not that interesting. No one is staring (unless you're possibly wearing a flamboyant hat, in which case people probably are) and no one is throwing you a pity party—they're too busy being absorbed with their own worries, issues, and food allergies.

It's quite mature and sophisticated to eat alone. You get to choose the place, the wine, and whether you want to stay for another thirty minutes to have dessert. And actually, rather than being mean, your waiter will probably spoil you—a solo diner is far easier than a raucous gaggle of twelve.

I have started eating out alone in the past few years, when traveling around the world *toute seule* meant I had to face my fear or eat a lot of club sandwiches on my hotel bed. I take a book or magazine and a confident swagger, and boy, have I eaten well! And I get to truly relish a fine meal without any drama.

The best part is that if you dine alone, you don't have to share the chocolate soufflé!

DON'T JUST TAKE IT FROM ME . . .

"I actually prefer eating on my own because I'm nearly always watching what I eat. With friends, I'll get my arm twisted into ordering extra sides or sharing a bottle of wine, which makes me feel sluggish the next day. On my own, I can order the nutritious stuff I like without my friends moaning that I am boring."

Karen, 32, shipping associate, Miami

"It's easy to imagine you'd be viewed as a friendless freak for eating out alone, especially somewhere very posh and date night–ish. But the truth is, once you start doing it, you become aware of all the other solo diners out there. Why should I go without a steak from my favorite place after a bad day in the office because my buddies are busy?"

Elizabeth, 38, medical sales rep, Atlanta

Still enjoy your food! Spend time cooking the stuff you see being cooked on your favorite television show. Don't just sit there watching these wonderful cooks at work while eating prepackaged food heated up in the microwave. Buy a few books and get into the kitchen. Cooking is easier than you think and is a real stress reliever. Or go to a diner and order the cheapest thing on the menu. Those stools at the counter were designed for solo customers, and no one will give you a second glance. Just order up and enjoy having the time all to yourself.

8 Buy Your Own Jewelry

It can seem as if women have sucked up all the bad stuff that comes with working like a man: long hours, nasty bosses, prematurely gray hair, and heart attacks. We're working harder and longer, and still—as research shows—when in a relationship, it's women who are expected to do the majority of cooking, cleaning, and child care.

To deal with all this tough stuff, we need a bit of twinkle, and why oh why should we wait for a man to deem us worthy of it?

If you need some sparkle, satisfy yourself and spend your own cash—as long as you have it. There is something very modern about treating yourself to your own rocks. I can't deny there is something magical about being given jewelry by a loved one, be it an eternity ring from your man or a family heirloom from your parents. But likewise, there is something marvelous about treating yourself: showing the world you have worked hard and you love yourself for it.

So if there isn't someone lurking in the wings with a promising-looking ring box, sod it. Buy yourself a treat—you've probably got better taste anyway.

DON'T JUST TAKE IT FROM ME . . .

"My fiancé broke off our engagement last year, and for a good few months I just couldn't take off my ring. When I finally did, my hands looked dull and old. So I took the money I was going to spend on my wedding dress and took myself to Cartier to buy a Russian wedding ring. It's beautiful, and every time I look at my fingers I know how far I've come."

Kaye, 36, teacher, San Diego

"I admire myself when I buy stuff—I saved up, I worked hard, I don't give men control. One thing you should wait for a guy to do is pay for you to go on an experience. A hot-air balloon ride is more authentic and real—and will say more about your relationship—than a rock."

Chloe, 26, accountant, New York City

IF YOU CAN'T BUY YOURSELF JEWELRY . . .

Think about what other treats will be a constant reminder that you have value and merit. For some women it's shoes; others simply indulge in a stack of their favorite magazines every Saturday morning. Whatever you choose, don't get hung up on the fact you're indulging. Your rewards are justified.

9 Have as Many First Kisses as Your Morals Allow

Who doesn't love that intense feeling of electricity you get when you know someone is about to kiss you? The tremble starts from your knees and works its way all the way up, through your naughty bits and into your fuzzy brain. Ooh, I feel quite light-headed just thinking about it.

The best first-kiss story I've heard is from a dear writer friend of mine, who was lucky enough to have a very juicy moment with an A-list actor. So here they are at the usual Hollywood shindig. There's champagne, not much to eat, and lots of talk of scripts while rubbernecking. The hunky star walks in. He really is as jaw-droppingly handsome as he looks in the movies—and taller than my friend imagined, so this is all good. Every woman in the room wants a bit of the action but my friend has an excuse to talk to him: she's recently started working for his agent. She struts over, hoping he can't hear her beating heart, and strikes up a conversation. He's friendly and has an irresistible twinkle in his eyes. She's besotted.

To her great delight, he talks to her all evening, protectively pulling her against a wall and leaning into her when fans and wannabes get in their way.

After a few hours of intense eye contact and arm touching, my friend, fueled by the champagne bubbles, summons the courage to ask, "So are you going to kiss me?" As the words fall out of her mouth, she regrets it. What has she done? He is a hugely famous, gorgeous film star and she is being cockily forward!

He leans in. She could feel his lips against her ear and his firm body close to hers as he says, "We've been kissing all night—our lips just haven't been touching." And then they kiss, and kiss, and kiss some more (she had quite the stubble rash the next day). They ended up dating, he turned out to be a promiscuous asshole, so they finished, and she's had hundreds more first kisses since then.

Kissing is very intimate, but it's not like you're jumping into bed with every Tom, Dick, and Harry you meet—you're simply playing tonsil tennis. As long as you are single, you should never get too hung up about appearing too frisky or flirty. Have fun and snog your little socks off. Embrace your singledom and those rare moments of mutual attraction while you can.

DON'T JUST TAKE IT FROM ME . . .

"Once you're married, you can never make out with anyone else ever again, so do it now. It's good because you realize how many good, and how many bad, kissers there are. I've had a disturbing one who licked my face once. You'll be happy to marry a good kisser when you find him and don't have to go through bad ones again."

Charlotte, 30, publishing executive, Medford, Massachusetts

"I used to kiss lots of boys—I had my time. Now that I've got a fiancé, I'm glad I did, because I can't have first kisses anymore. I had friends who wouldn't kiss lots of boys because I think they just thought it was silly or slutty, but they will regret that down the line, I know."

Amber, 24, preschool teacher, San Diego

IF YOU CAN'T HAVE MANY FIRST KISSES . . .

Get your passion fix in the pages of romance novels. We all need that heart-swelling, knee-crumbling feeling sometimes. It reminds us we're emotionally alive. Don't be ashamed to cry your heart out during a romantic movie, either.

10 Learn to Cook Something Exceptional

We can't all be top chefs, but we can all learn a little from just spending some hours in the kitchen. I'm not talking about rolling your own sushi or making a crème brûlée—necessarily. But every fabulous girl should have a signature dish to wow guests and prospective in-laws alike.

I'm not a natural in the kitchen. In fact, since moving to New York I haven't used my oven once (I use it to store shoes) and have clicked on the microwave only a couple of times to pop some corn. But if push came to shove, I have a trick up my sleeve: a mean moussaka, which I learned to make ten years ago and has been wowing the palates of my pals ever since. I don't mean to blow my own trumpet, but it's delicious. This proves we can all cook. It just takes time and patience.

Don't throw yourself into the deep end, preparing a four-course dinner party for your boss. Take it slowly. This is where the *learn to cook something— one thing—exceptional* comes in. If your pièce de résistance is sublime enough, no one will notice the shop-bought appetizer and the ice cream you throw onto the table for dessert. Ask your mum—or a friend who also happens to be a domestic goddess—for a few family recipes. Get her to donate an afternoon to teaching you how to make something delicious and simple, and write everything down as you go. Stick to good, plain ingredients that will be easy to find all year-round and won't break the bank to buy. One friend gave me a tip that wrapping plain chicken breasts in streaky bacon makes them look and taste more impressive. And served with a mustard and onion gravy on a bed of mashed potatoes, this dish has quickly become a winter comfort food my friends know to ask for on cold evenings. If you haven't got someone on hand to help, nestle in with a notepad and the Food Network. If you think something sounds delicious, chances are your friends will, too. Do a practice run, then try it out a few times. If it goes well, it won't be long before word gets around that your dish is exceptional and your dinner parties become the place to be.

DON'T JUST TAKE IT FROM ME . . .

"I work long hours but I still love to have a life during the week. So I've become salmon lady. It's the easiest thing in the world to prepare, but because fish is considered quite a treat, my friends feel spoiled when I exit my kitchen clutching it. Wrapped in foil and doused in fresh lemon juice and capers, the salmon—served with salad and crusty bread—has become my signature dish. Easy but delicious."

Andrea, 32, marketing coordinator,
New York City

"I have a sweet tooth and quickly found out after I got married that desserts were the only thing that could hold my interest long enough to keep me in the kitchen. Luckily, my husband likes the sweet stuff, too . . . He now thinks he's married to Rachael Ray because I keep the cakes coming while his dinners come from the frozen-food section of the supermarket."

Danielle, 28, photo researcher, Boston

IF YOU CAN'T MAKE ONE EXCEPTIONAL DISH . . .

Learn to cheat well. Investigate the prepared meals at your local supermarket but use garnishes to give them that home-cooked spin. Add herbs, sauces, seasonings, and dressings. Bring out freshly warm bread from the oven (yes, you bought that, too, but heating up a loaf for a few minutes pleases the most fussy food connoisseur). Voilà!

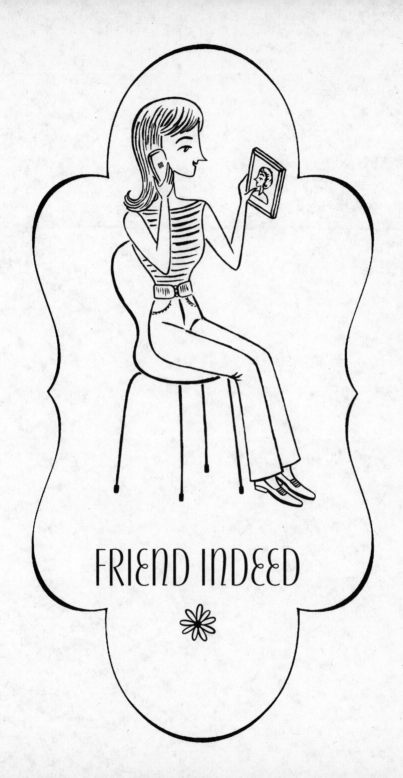

FRIEND INDEED

11 Compete with Yourself, Not Your Girlfriends

At school, I could get quite jealous of people who were more popular than me. I was envious of the girls who got to date the boys I liked. Certainly in my first couple of jobs, I didn't understand why some of my peers—who weren't as enthusiastic or conscientious as I was—were my boss's favorites while I was left out on the sidelines.

My self-confidence would crumble, and I'd gossip about my supposed rivals, unleashing a side of me that made me feel horrid. Being in bitter competition with others could make me a bitch. But I wasn't naturally a bitch, and I decided I certainly wasn't going to become one for the sake of a promotion or the cheap thrill of popularity.

I resolved at the age of twenty-three to stop feeling these dark and damaging emotions of jealousy and rivalry and to focus on beating my own standards and setting my own targets. Life is a long race, and you should be competing only against yourself, or rather your *better you.* I stopped looking out and started looking in.

I still feel the occasional twinge of jealousy, obviously. I'm not a saint. When those feelings emerge, I face them directly and try to learn from the person whose possession I covet. Convert your jealousy into a desire to observe and absorb the allure in other people. People will sense it and offer you more—rather than feel threatened.

Now when people try to compete with me, their negative energy hits me in the solar plexus as though they've thrown a punch. A sly comment or a subtle undermining—either makes me aware in a "friendly" manner that someone has been gossiping about me. It's all nasty stuff, but instead of dragging me down as it once would have, I continue on my path and know that karma will win out.

Buddha's last words were "Strive on diligently." These are words I take seriously. We should all push toward our own personal goals with passion and determination, not rest on our laurels when we've gotten ahead of the person standing next to us or when we're earning more than our colleagues at work. We should continue to strive for our own hopes and dreams, looking around us only for inspiration and advice, never to crow or boast. Push yourself to beat the clock on the treadmill during your morning run, challenge yourself to finish a book a week, reward yourself with a treat if you stick to your path of healthy eating for a month, but keep your friends and co-workers out of it. There are people who get ahead in life by being the best they can be, and there are people who get ahead in life by putting down and climbing on other people. Which do you want to be?

DON'T JUST TAKE IT FROM ME . . .

"I used to be a very competitive sort. I was always bitter that I didn't earn as much as my friends but was working longer hours or that I wasn't being rewarded for my effort and brains when people around me seemed to be. It was making me depressed. It wasn't until I stopped looking outward, but inward, that my luck seemed to change—and suddenly I was the one getting the pay raises."

Jill, 32, computer programmer, Columbus, Ohio

"Laid-back, that's me. In all areas except love. When it comes to my exes, I'm super competitive. At work, I can congratulate others and don't think about moaning if the boss prefers someone else. But if I see an ex has a new girlfriend on Facebook and she's slimmer than me, forget it. Steam comes out of my ears. I need to work on that. The negative energy is bad for my health!"

*Arabella, 27, personal assistant,
Sacramento, California*

IF YOU CAN'T BE IN COMPETITION ONLY
WITH YOURSELF . . .

Let your jealousy and competitive spirit spur you on to improve your own situation—and be open about it. "I wish I had your job. How did you get the promotion?" Talk to those you envy. Aspire to be like them instead of wasting time bitching about them. As much as you're looking ahead to what you want next, someone else will be behind you, thinking you've got something worth being envious of, too!

12 Get Creative with Your Giving

Too often, we associate generosity with money. We mistakenly think we can buy people with material kindness—a huge birthday present or perhaps an extra round of drinks at the bar. This is all very well and good, of course, but it's the meaning behind our generosity that really matters.

As you go through life, you will find yourself in different financial situations from those around you. Peer pressure grows as we hit our teens and twenties, and the need to display our generosity can cause massive problems. But this is entirely avoidable. I don't know about you, but the gifts I have remembered the most are those that have shown a true level of thoughtfulness, not the ones that have cost the most.

It's better to give with our time and our hearts, not just our wallets. Gifts are not worth getting yourself into debt over. And you should never feel embarrassed by admitting to people around you that "hey, I'm saving up for an apartment/vacation/dental work; I can come out to dinner tonight, but can we just pay for ourselves or go somewhere reasonable that fits my budget?"

This isn't being mean or tightfisted—this is being realistic.

A great way to show generosity without spending too much is to write IOUs: IOU a home-cooked meal, IOU a girlie video night and popcorn, IOU a foot massage and pedicure . . . I've had a few friends give me these, and they're fabulous and fun. Get creative with your giving, and remember, often the most wonderful thing you can give another person is your positive energy. To help you get in the spirit I recommend the book *The Celestine Prophecy* by James Redfield, which discusses how we can build one another up and make the world beautiful by generously donating our love and time and good vibes. Be known as a truly generous person, not just a person who can afford to splash out on big gifts.

DON'T JUST TAKE IT FROM ME . . .

"Diamonds can be a girl's best friend, but to be honest, I've loved more the personal presents men have given me: a book of poetry that he knew I'd love, a special photo, a surprise trip. None of these things compares financially with those big, shiny rocks, but they do compare in heartfelt generosity."

Susannah, 35, personal trainer, Dallas

"There's no shame in saving. I've learned the hard way that being too generous because I was embarrassed means trouble. Pleasing a bunch of fake friends wasn't worth the bad credit-card debt I accumulated. Your true buddies love you for you, not your paycheck!"

Christina, 34, bank manager, New York City

IF YOU CAN'T GET CREATIVE WITH YOUR
GENEROSITY . . .

Pick your moments! Sometimes you'll have more disposable income than at other times. So set up a savings account to which you can make regular contributions for gifts and cards, or when you do have a little extra money, send your favorite people a gift as a surprise. I love sending people gifts in the post just because. These gifts are more appreciated because they highlight that I wanted my friends to have something special or that I was just thinking of them, not that my generosity was expected because of a date on the calendar.

13 Listen to the Warning Bells

When my mother got ready to marry my father at the age of twenty-five, she knew something wasn't quite right. She heard warning bells. Every time he let her down, made her feel worthless, flirted with other women, or didn't fulfill a promise, she heard these bells.

Her mother—my grandmother—asked her about these bells. Did they always happen at the same time, in the same sort of situation? Did she know what these bells meant?

Deep down, of course, my mother did, but she didn't want to listen. She wanted a husband (a charming, handsome husband at that), and she wanted her dream: a normal life with a house, a man, security, and eventually some children. Despite her own inner wisdom and her mother's probing words, she covered her ears and hummed over the increasing ringing in her head.

Why didn't she listen to the bells? She simply chose not to. However, the next time those bells started ringing—a few years into her marriage and his nastiness—she recognized the sound. Within those few years, my mother had got one wish (me!) but lost all her others. Her charming, handsome husband turned out to be a philandering liar. And although by that time she had a baby and a six-year-old to support, she listened to the chimes and told him to leave. She embraced the bells, and our little family was much better off for it.

Every woman gets these alarms at times of great risk or distraction, even about small things: Do you really need that third bar of chocolate? Are you hungry as your stomach is saying, or are you depressed as that tinkling in your head is suggesting? Now I stop, contemplate, and listen whenever something doesn't sound quite right. I get a vibe off some people that I pay attention to, and some say I am a good judge of character. We all have the potential—everyone just needs to embrace what her soul is trying to say, through voices, through gut instinct, through warning bells.

DON'T JUST TAKE IT FROM ME . . .

"I was in a job for seven years and I got comfortable and lazy, despite it making me unhappy. Then there were whispers of changes and redundancies and the atmosphere got even worse, but still I stayed—even when I was offered a new job. Despite my heart telling me to make the leap, I stayed put, persuading myself I didn't have the energy for something new. When everything at the company fell apart and I was forced to leave, I chastised myself for not listening to the warning bells. I'm happy now, but it's taken me years to feel secure again."

Rudisha, 34, makeup artist, San Francisco

"Last fall I was starting to look for a fresh challenge at work and was offered two different positions. One I wanted straightaway—it was perfect—but my boss wanted me to take the other one. I gave in, even though in my head I knew I'd be happier in the other job. I didn't follow my own instincts and I wish I had. I took his advice, which he'd given selfishly, and I've paid for it. Heed the bells!"

Julia, 35, software project manager, Rochester, New York

IF YOU CAN'T LISTEN TO WARNING BELLS . . .

Find a trustworthy friend who has only your best interests at heart. He or she can act as your conscience and guide you to the right end when you feel stuck in the mud. This friend should not be a colleague (professional jealousy could arise) or someone in the same romantic situation as you (she may push you to leave a relationship in order to test the waters for a singleton before she does the same or put you off a good guy because she doesn't want to be the only one left on the shelf). You will recognize an honest heart when you find one.

NO REGRETS

14 Finish Unfinished Business

Everyone has something niggling away at her that consciously or unconsciously stops her from fully embracing life—and sometimes from enjoying a good night's sleep. Without facing up to it and taking action, you will continue to be haunted by this unfinished business.

These can be tiny little things that no one else would notice or big things the world is waiting for you to acknowledge. Let me give you examples of both, the little one first.

Recently on a vacation, a strapping lad helped carry my luggage to my room. I assumed he was a bellboy whose uniform was at the dry cleaners, so I gave him a tip. Cringe! I found out soon after he was a fellow guest with a helpful attitude who liked the look of me (and I wonder why I'm single!). For days, I hid behind the palm trees when I saw him approach. Eventually, distressed by the inability to get a suntan while lurking in shrubbery, I decided to apologize. He laughed and said, "No, seriously, thanks for the money—it bought me a beer! You're a good tipper." We laughed it off, and I felt silly for carrying such a minor offense around with me for so long.

After my divorce, I found out one of my university boyfriends—the one I had thought of as the heartbreaker who should give me a second chance—was also newly divorced and single. I tracked him down and arranged to meet him one night. I was lonely and wanted to see if any of the electricity remained.

I spent ages getting ready for the date—a haircut, new dress, lots of imaginary conversations in my head—and then there he was in front of me. A slightly chubbier, balder version of the guy I liked all those years ago. We both drank steadily to squash our nerves and I realized with great sadness that he hadn't amounted to much. He still relied on his father's money, had never pushed himself into a career, and had never even bothered to get his driver's license. What a disappointment this college Romeo had turned out to be.

We kissed at the end of the night, because that's what you do when you're single, tipsy, and with a man you once fancied, but the spark was gone and I couldn't wait to leave. I wished him well and turned away, knowing I would never see him again.

For a few days, I had mixed emotions about our meeting. Would it have been better to never have met, to have lived forever with a fantasy of what could have been? But then I realized that if I was still hankering after him, no other man could have the whole of my heart, and that finishing that bit of unfinished business was probably the healthiest thing I could have done for myself and the *real* man of my dreams.

DON'T JUST TAKE IT FROM ME . . .

"You need to get closure, and sometimes that means being the bigger person and saying sorry first or asking the difficult questions first. Even if they acted terribly and you acted appropriately, rely on your own sense of self-esteem to iron out stressful situations. Life is short. Time is condensed. In your twenties you think you have plenty of time to forget things or make the most of people and that you can deal with stuff later. You can't. Do it now."

Hillarie, 38, marketing consultant, New York City

"When my mother was dying, I did everything I could, everything in my power, to make her last days happy. I drove for five hours every Monday to see her and talk to her about her life. It was tiring, but when she eventually passed away, I knew I'd pleased her and I could have nothing to regret. But I have siblings who didn't deal with the situation very well and didn't spend time with her before she died. When someone dies, there is no going back. Finish your business with someone important while you can."

Jane, 61, developer, Annapolis, Maryland

IF YOU CAN'T FINISH YOUR UNFINISHED BUSINESS...

At least try to own the situation in your mind. Don't push it to the back of your head. It will come back to haunt you. If a person or situation is bothering you but you feel you cannot confront the cause, talk to a therapist or a good friend about it. Remember: a problem shared is a problem halved.

15 Love Your Family— Conventional or Not

The days of the stay-at-home mom, strong dad, 2.4 children, and family dog are long gone. Thankfully we are now more open about what constitutes a family. But our modern idea of a family can include people the law wouldn't consider as such: friends, neighbors, even exes.

I want to emphasize that a true, loving family is the one you choose and make. No matter what circumstances you were born into, everyone deserves a close network of people who will love and support her.

When I first moved to America from England, I didn't know anyone. It was a lonely time, and for a good few months I hid my loneliness by working 24/7 and surrounding myself with photos of my family and friends back home. But that was no way to live. I slowly started to meet people, and I realized that most of them were like me: thrown into this big city for work reasons, with their families miles away. We decided to become one another's new family, and from them I got the best bits of family life: support, trust, friendship, and someone to call if I had a problem who would invite me round for a cup of tea.

Families. You can't live with them and you can't live without them. But if someone is offering you love, a home, and/or his or her name, even if you are not from the same gene pool, be gracious and grateful.

And people, in this day of remarriage and confused lineage, you're going to have to accept waifs and strays into your precious family. Do so with an open, honest heart. Blood may be thicker, but water is refreshing, satisfying, and clean.

DON'T JUST TAKE IT FROM ME . . .

"Don't force yourself to follow family rituals if they don't strengthen you as a person. Family members may be blood relations, but that doesn't automatically mean they have your best interests at heart. I now have a pact with my husband. If we don't want to go, then we don't. We visit friends instead."

Donna, 49, technical consultant, San Jose

"My sister and I were adopted as young children, and in my teen years—when I first uncovered this fact—I was confused and angry about not being wanted by my real parents. My sister had a different reaction. She saw it that we were desperately wanted by another couple who weren't linked to us by blood—just a desire to love children. She has inspired me to be thankful every day for my unconventional family unit."

Keren, 31, jewelry buyer, Little Rock

IF YOU DO THINK BLOOD IS THICKER THAN WATER . . .

Open your mind. Every family—however it's composed—deserves praise when the family is bound by love and respect.

16 Explore Religious Teachings from a Tradition You Weren't Raised In

Fundamentally, all religions want and require the same thing: contemplation, kindness, respect, and a humble heart. What's wrong with that? Whatever book you read it in, whatever language you are preached at in, the principles are the same: be good, be fair, and help others.

We should all embrace the different philosophies and teachings of our friends' religions, perhaps even go to a service or two, to see what we can learn from them. Why limit yourself to one set of rules when generations and generations of good thoughts and beliefs are on offer to us? You will most likely find your own truth—and get stronger convictions of right or wrong—through religious education.

I still find that parents put unnecessary pressure on their offspring to stick with a certain religious group—and certainly to not marry outside of it. Open your eyes to the world, the people of the world, and all the things you can learn from them. We may be on different paths, but ultimately we should all have the same goal: to live a happy and fulfilled life complete with love and kindness. Learn different religious teachings through books and letters, through visiting places of worship, and through talking to your friends about their traditions.

Educate yourself to know more about your prejudices. Raised Church of England, I rebelled a while ago and turned toward Buddhism as a way to live my life. The more I read, the more I learned that Jesus and the Bible have some pretty cool stories that aren't too far from what Buddha taught. I could easily marry both practices. Take the best of all of these ancient teachings, and ignore the bits that don't fit with you and your modern life.

DON'T JUST TAKE IT FROM ME . . .

"I grew up Eastern Orthodox, and since my father was an engineer for NYC Transit Authority, which was the immigrant express at the time, I was exposed to all religions. His best friends were Hindu, Muslim, and Baptist. My best friends are Muslim, Catholic, Protestant, Jewish, Orthodox, etc. We can sometimes spend hours debating politics and religion, often accompanied by copious amounts of Turkish coffee."

Olga, 44, artist, New York City

"In college, I had an assignment to attend the Zion Baptist Church for a Sunday morning service. I'm Presbyterian, which means no clapping, standing, or speaking out of turn during the succinct hour-long service. I wasn't prepared for the four-hour, singing, dancing, spirit-filled Zion Baptist service. I love my church, but I was so impressed that I've never forgotten that day. Everyone should try a new experience at least once. There's a lot to learn and appreciate."

—Hallie, editorial assistant, New York City

Analyze your own and actually think about it. Decide which mantras and lessons to take with you through this life and which of the dogmas you can live without.

17 Express Gratitude

Sorry can be the hardest word to say, but often a simple *thank you* is tricky, too. Does expressing gratitude reveal a certain weakness or neediness?

When others show generosity or kindness, I don't believe they are doing so for the thanks, but you cannot underestimate the power of a smile or a friendly word on someone else's day. Have you ever held a door open for someone to walk through without receiving a word of thanks? How did you feel? As though you shouldn't have bothered, right? Capture that brief glimmer of *grrrr* and decide you shall never put a fellow good-mannered person in that situation.

A thank-you note is the next level of loveliness; a phone call is also a treat. Be sure to make a note of birthday and Christmas gifts so you know whom to thank and for what among the debris of wrapping paper.

For the really big events in life, when someone has been there for you, you should express gratitude on deeper levels than words. And I'm not talking about financially—sure, a bottle of wine could be nice for the recipient, and if you have the cash, splash it—but I mean expressing thanks by listening to her advice, taking her words on board, and appreciating her friendship. If someone goes out of her way for you, you need to acknowledge it.

You should also express gratitude to yourself. Everything you are or have become is a reflection of your strength, your wisdom, and your journey. So stop and say thank you in the mirror every now and again, and reward yourself. Treat yourself to chocolate, a massage, an early night. If you've had a tough day, thank yourself for the hard work by taking a long bubble bath.

It costs nothing to smile. It costs nothing to express gratitude. Treat others how you would like to be treated and you can't go wrong.

DON'T JUST TAKE IT FROM ME . . .

"If there's someone in your life who has taught you a lot of high value, be sure to tell that person, because you'll wish you did when it's too late. I had a role model in my career that I learned a lot from. When he retired, I told him, "Thank you for coming into my life." It meant a lot to him, and I have had a lot of success in my career based on the things that he taught me. And accept gratitude with good grace. It is nice to receive. Don't say your kind gesture was nothing. It wasn't."

Jill, 45, teacher, Cleveland

"When I was a teenager and young adult, I was so shy I couldn't say thank you—I couldn't say a word. Last year, I made a conscious decision to be kinder, more cognizant of people and their feelings. I learned to verbalize my thankfulness for little things and big things. As soon as I started saying thanks, people's

attitudes toward me changed and the negative energy around
me has become positive. A great thing."

Christine, 43, public affairs, Calgary

IF YOU CAN'T EXPRESS GRATITUDE . . .

Practice. Investigate further. Why are you so scared of
showing vulnerability or accepting help from others?
Are you painfully shy or just downright rude? If it's
the latter, tsk-tsk—learn some etiquette. Even if po-
liteness doesn't come naturally, once you see how
people's attitudes toward you change, you'll be encouraged to make good manners a part of your life.
And if you're just too proud, get over yourself. It's
okay to need help—we all do at some point. Just make
sure you appreciate it.

18 Be Nice to Your Friends' Love Interests

This might be harder than you think. To you, your
friend is smart, witty, and beautiful, and she deserves
someone of equal good standing—this guy just may
not be good enough for her. But life doesn't unfold
like a Jane Austen novel where everyone is perfectly
matched off, like for like.

Perhaps her new man has hidden charms: he may
not have the best job in the world, but maybe he runs
her a bath after a stressful day and makes sure he's always got her favorite ice cream in the freezer. Before

you judge him unworthy, try to see what she sees in him.

Another possible reason you may not approve of her lustful paramour is that—dare we admit it?—you're jealous. You're single (or even worse, stuck in a disintegrating relationship), and her new happiness is like a kick in the teeth. You want her to be a little bit lonely like you. That way, you'll always have someone to go to the cinema with on Saturday nights.

Well, get over it. I've been in both situations and neither is healthy; being nice to the random men who come in and out of friends' lives takes a lot less energy than disapproving of them. Tell him the kind things your friend says about him, ask him about his job, show an interest in his sports teams. Just be nice. And if you are single, befriend him so you can get access to all his single mates. Give an opinion to your girlfriend if asked, but remember: she could marry this guy! He could be around forever, and your negativity is more likely to force a wedge between you and your friend than between the happy couple.

DON'T JUST TAKE IT FROM ME . . .

"My whole group hated our friend's boyfriend. He had this disgusting habit of blowing his nose on his sleeve, and if he ever did have a tissue, he'd leave the snot rags all over the place. It made us want to gag. We brought his dirty habit up in a jokey way, knowing she was besotted, and because we did it so delicately, she didn't go mental. She had a word with him; he stopped . . . And now we can appreciate his silly, soft, charming side that she sees."

Joanna, 28, dancer, New York City

"I couldn't see the charm in my best friend's boyfriend at all—and to start with, I didn't give him the time of day. But eventually, I realized that he was so good to her, her happiness was something we both cherished, and I respected him. We're not friends now, but I have to say I like him. And really, it's good I don't find him charming and I'm not secretly lusting after him. Now, *that* would damage our friendship!"

Katie, 29, waitress, Kentwood, Louisiana

IF YOU CAN'T BE NICE TO YOUR FRIENDS' LOVE INTERESTS ...

There are two different methods to deal with this: (1) Remove yourself from the situation completely, or (2) If there is something that rubs you the wrong way about him, take advice from neutral people around you. Lay the facts on the table and ask them to help you decide if you are acting out of self-interest or in your friend's interest. If he really is a cad who needs to go, tell her once—without judgement—and then let her decide.

19 Keep Close Friends Close

I never thought it would happen, but suddenly my childhood girlfriends and I are all grown up and running off in different directions. I threw the first spanner in the works, of course, by leaving London and moving to New York. Since then some of my friends have had children and it's hard to keep in touch even more.

It's strange that after years of sharing and caring and getting through tricky teen patches of jealousy and insecurity, we can find ourselves distant from the ones we love the most.

Finding common ground—and the time to discuss it—can feel like a chore, but it is worth the effort. Friends are like reflections of ourselves, highlighting where we want to be, want not to be, or dream to be one day. I've found it tough adjusting to my close friends' pregnancies. Rather than letting these friends fall out of my life, I'm trying to do what they did when I upped and moved four thousand miles away. I'm admiring their bravery, staying interested in their news, and spending time reminiscing about all of our happy moments together.

We grow up, we change, and our values shift, but good friends should be able to weather these storms of distance and lifestyle changes. In twenty years' time, when the kids are grown up, we'll need someone to have a giggle with. As therapist Elizabeth Foley so elegantly put it, "The most beautiful discovery true friends make is that they can grow separately without growing apart."

DON'T JUST TAKE IT FROM ME . . .

"My best friend has become a different person since having her first child. All she talks about is him, she won't come out on girls' night anymore, and she thinks anyone who is not a mother is wasting her life. But I'm being patient. I know her so well—that underneath her new judgments is a woman scared of failing. I'll be there for her when she wants to open up."

Gina, 32, realtor, Trenton, New Jersey

"My best friend from school came out a few years ago, and we both found it really tough. Obviously, she was the one with the massive traumas and changes to go through—but I did think about how it would change our relationship. People's circumstances change, but the people are still the same deep down. We now go to lesbian bars one week and out on a manhunt the next. It's made me much more open in all areas of my life, and I'm grateful for that."

Susie, 32, teacher, Los Angeles

IF YOU CAN'T KEEP THOSE FRIENDS CLOSE . . .

Move on with the hope you will be friends again—but don't become friendless while you wait. Make new friends who share more with you at this point in your life. Accept drinks with colleagues after work and organize a healthy vacation with your Pilates-class chums.

20 Give an Ex-boyfriend a Second Chance . . . But Not a Third

When I split up with a boyfriend, I feel as if my heart is being ripped out while my stomach is being punched in. It's not nice, this end-of-love thang.

That must be why, dear reader, it is so tempting to give an ex a second chance. Dating is hard. We all have a list of criteria in our head of what we want our partner to be, and the fact that you used to go out with this chap means he must have had your desired qualities at some point. Meanwhile, the new men you meet are too short, egocentric, uncommunicative, lazy, poor, unstable—yada yada yada.

So when the ex calls you after a few months and says he misses you and he's changed, your heart practically leaps out of your chest and runs round to his apartment. After feeling heavy behind your rib cage for such a long time, it's longing to be held for a little while. An ex seems like the easy, comfortable option. You've tried new men—hell, you've even slept with a few—but you don't know your way around their idiosyncrasies (or their bodies) yet and it's all a bit too much like hard work.

So you take the ex back into your arms—and life. He says he's changed, and he's certainly appearing grateful and humble. He calls you when he says he's going to, shows up on time, even buys you flowers, and seems to listen to what you're saying without gazing off into the distance or at some hot chick. This is fantastic. The risk paid off.

But did it? Keep an eye on how things progress. Avoid slipping into the old patterns. You both have to work very hard to stop falling back into the ruts and routines that made you both miserable in the first place. Keep up with your girlfriends, keep the hobbies you took up while you were lonely, keep going away for mini breaks and vacations (even though you'd secretly rather spend the weekend in bed with him). Stay independent this time, just in case he breaks your heart again. He may be the one and he may have changed, but you are older and wiser and you should act it. And if he treats you badly again, let that be the end of it. Everyone deserves a second chance, but someone who neglects your feelings and doesn't put you first does not deserve a third.

DON'T JUST TAKE IT FROM ME . . .

"If the relationship has come to a bitter end twice before, why risk a third? I took my ex back twice after he cheated on me, and by taking him back those times he felt like he could screw me over even worse. The third time was the most devastating of all. I still can't get over what a painful breakup that was for me, even though it was ten years ago and I'm married with three beautiful children. You can't teach an old dog new tricks."

Maria, 34, photo director, Hoboken, New Jersey

"A year after I split with my boyfriend, he began to call and write and beg for a second chance. I kept him waiting for six months. I wanted to see if his heart was really in it or whether he was just going through a dating dry spell and I was the easy option. Since the day I agreed to see him again, he has made every effort to make it work. And we are making it work. He is aware that if he ever treats me badly again, he won't be getting another chance."

Barbra, 34, doctor, Philadelphia

IF YOU CAN'T RESIST TAKING YOUR EX BACK A THIRD TIME . . .

Don't expect your family and friends to be as supportive and sympathetic as they were the first and second times he broke your heart. Sometimes it's easy to look upon a situation with clarity when you are not in the middle of it. The people who love you will probably see he's not right for you and he's going to hurt you again while you're still blissfully holed up in cloud cuckoo land. If you must give it a third shot, make him work for it. He had better treat you like a princess, sister; otherwise his karma is going to get him in the end. Hooray.

21 Ditch Toxic Friends

Good friends are hard to come by. True, loyal, energetic, kind, thoughtful, and fun friends are even harder. I've worked hard to keep my close relationships because friends are what make the world go round.

Bad friends can make your world slow down. A good buddy of mine, James Arthur Ray (the handsome expert from *The Secret* and rock star of personal transformation), taught me a lot about this. His whole philosophy is that some friends are toxic, and although they'd never admit it, they'd love to put you down, keep you down, and make you feel generally down about yourself. This doesn't make them nasty. It makes them human.

As soon as you start taking charge of your life, embracing challenges, being brave, fighting for your corner, and improving your life, some people around you won't be able to handle it. You become a walking, talking, breathing reminder of everything they should be achieving. The minute a friend starts turning on you because your diet is going well and you've lost ten pounds, or you've gotten a promotion at work, or you've got a hot new boyfriend who adores you, understand that this says more about her than you—and don't doubt yourself and what you're doing.

You have to take control of the situation before the nastiness eats away at your spirit. At first, try the confrontational approach. Say, "I know you're having trouble with the changes going on, but I am your friend and you are mine. Please support me (and cut out the backstabbing)."

If the up-front approach doesn't work and your friend doesn't change her behavior toward you, she needs to look at herself and you need to get new friends.

It sounds harsh, but it's true. When you move on to and wish to maintain a higher level, you need to be with like-minded, happy, healthy, confident people. Not those embittered with anger and aggression toward you.

As you move forward, you will naturally attract these people, and soon your cell phone or Facebook page will be full of interesting, encouraging new friends.

DON'T JUST TAKE IT FROM ME . . .

"Don't question yourself too harshly. If a friend turns on you, ask yourself, 'Have I done anything to harm her?' If the answer is no, ask yourself, 'Have I done anything good for myself that she could be jealous of?' I bet you there is something, and I promise you that's why she's turned bitchy."

Clare, 33, stylist, Dublin

"I have one friend who was very clever with her snide remarks. I didn't notice for the longest time—in fact, it was new friends who pointed it out. It was silly things that would undermine my confidence. Giggling at me in the changing room when I went shopping for a new outfit, or when I'd mention that a boy had a crush on me, denying it by stating he was obviously gay. I was feeling quite down on myself until I took her power away by breaking our bond."

Francis, 25, waitress, Omaha, Nebraska

IF YOU CAN'T DITCH BAD FRIENDSHIPS . . .

Take control. See these people only when you fancy it, and switch off your phone if you suspect they're lurking about. Stand up for yourself and tell toxic folks to be a good friend. The relationship might still be a cross you have to bear—but at least you won't have lost your self-respect.

22 Be the First to Apologize

Never is it more important to act quickly than when you have upset another human being—be it a friend, relation, or colleague—and you know you should apologize.

My oldest friend, Claire, is one of the loves of my life. She's a loyal, intelligent strawberry blond bombshell (we decided not to call her hair ginger) whom I have known since I was one year old in the nursery and hope to continue knowing for the rest of my life.

But when I was twenty-two I did a stupid thing, and it nearly cost me her companionship forever. I was a fledgling reporter for a tough London newspaper. I was doing anything I could to (a) impress my editor, and (b) simply survive.

I had an idea for a story about modern women and how they compared to their mothers' generation. What I deduced was that we were more materialistic, promiscuous, and ambitious. This all made for a great read—if I do say so myself—but the mistake I made was using Claire, who was my housemate at the time, as a case study. I hadn't yet learned that you shouldn't mix business with pleasure.

The article came out, and my jolly piece of fluff had been edited dramatically—Claire came across as a real snob. When she read it, everything went sour. She moved out, we lost touch, I resented her for confronting me, and we both went through lots of changes, trying to become new people who didn't need each other anymore.

It didn't work. I missed her. And I didn't like being a bitch. Eighteen months later—after little or no contact—I wrote her what can only be described as a love letter. I remember crying as I wrote it, begging her to see me so I could explain and telling her how I couldn't bear the thought of losing her friendship.

She got in touch immediately and my heart leaped for joy. We met and I apologized again. This gave her the power to apologize, too, for maybe blowing things out of proportion and for pushing other issues she had at the time onto me. We cried. We ate pizza and drank red wine. We cried some more and held hands.

Claire really is a soul mate, a sister, and my pride could have lost her to me forever. That letter is still the best letter I have ever written. And that meal is still one of the most memorable I've ever tasted.

DON'T JUST TAKE IT FROM ME . . .

"It's never too late to apologize. But if it could stop you from losing someone important in your life—even for just a few days—sooner is better than later. I was so stubborn in my early twenties, and I fell out with a close college pal because she stained a dress of mine. I didn't invite her to my wedding, and there's still someone missing when I look at the photos."

Kirsten, 26, writer, Long Beach, California

"I was quite nasty to a girl at school. She was the person I'd bash when I was feeling bad about myself. Eventually she rebelled and told me what she thought of me and how I'd hurt her confidence. It was hard to hear at the time, and I didn't apologize—I simply shut her out of my life. But I still feel guilty to this day."

Davina, 28, researcher, Trenton, New Jersey

IF YOU CAN'T BE THE FIRST TO APOLOGIZE . . .

Try harder. Pride is a difficult thing to push to one side. Normally in situations when an apology is needed, there are two sides to the story. Both parties may feel they are owed an apology. But if there is any gray area at all, own up to your mistake—even if you can do this only internally. Admit your faults to yourself and make a vow that you will never make such mistakes again.

23 Hear Your Mom Out

Mothers aren't perfect. Though I love her dearly, my mom manages to annoy me more than anyone else on the planet.

As I get older, the reason why she's able to get under my skin has become clear: she knows me better than anyone else. There's no bullshit. And because she knows me so well and has twenty-five years on me, she loves handing out advice. Sometimes it's easy to hear, but sometimes it makes me want to scream.

I remember being about fifteen and starting to develop a sense of, well, what I considered to be style. I was obsessed with the Smiths and the Cure, so I naturally aspired to their looks. My poor mom! No more Laura Ashley dresses or bouncy curls for me. I wore white powder to disguise my healthy glow and on one occasion drenched my golden locks in baby oil so I'd look suitably greasy and goth. Yuck.

As for my wardrobe, my mother was mortified when I insisted on wearing black leggings and Doc Martens boots on a weeklong beach holiday in Spain. She told me, "One day you're going to see photos of this time and wonder why such a pretty, slim young thing tried to make herself look so ugly!" I routinely shrugged and stuck my nose back into my book of Byronic verse. She was right. I'd love to be as slim and wrinkle free as I was in my teens. And I wasted it. In all the family photos from that five-year period, I look like Cousin Itt.

Hear your mother out. If she is still in your life, she loves you. She may not be perfect, but she loves you unconditionally, probably more than anyone else ever will for as long as you live.

DON'T JUST TAKE IT FROM ME . . .

"On a very serious occasion, I really should have heard my mother out: when I was twenty-two and announced I was getting married. She begged me not to, said I should trust her and that there was no need at such a young age to tie the knot. In an act of grand rebellion, I did it anyway. And guess what? Five years and an expensive divorce later, it finally sank in."

Courtney, 28, writer, Philadelphia, Pennsylvania

"My mom annoys me like no one else. One negative word from her cuts through me like a knife. It wasn't until I had my own child that I understood that the harshness and judgment were due to protection. I have a little boy, and I'm sure my lioness defense would be even worse if I had a little girl."

Amber, 32, senior director, New Orleans

IF YOU CAN'T HEAR YOUR MOM OUT . . .

Try to imagine what advice you would give your own daughter. This will lead to a sense of loving yourself and will help you to give good advice—and accept it—from a place of respect and kindness.

FASHIONISTA SISTA

24 Wear Your Sunday Best for All Occasions

Did anyone else's mother bark at her after any fancy family occasion to remove her special outfit as soon as possible and return to her bedroom in search of play clothes? Mine did. And, oh, how dismayed I was every time the pretty lace pinafore dress was restored to the wardrobe. Somewhere, the notion that my good clothes should be saved for only the nicest event sank in. In adulthood, if I treated myself to a cashmere sweater or fabulous pair of suede boots, instead of wearing it to my heart's content, I'd place it in a careful airtight spot in my closet and unwrap them only at times of utmost importance (a job interview, a friend's wedding, a first date with someone with whom I wanted to share a surname).

Then, hitting thirty, I read an interesting article that changed my way of thinking. It was a serious article about the cost of fashion—style mathematics, really. The author justified spending one thousand dollars on a dream handbag because, if you take that Mulberry leatherwork satchel (ooh, surely every girl's dream) to work every day for a year, it works out to about four dollars per day. If that gorgeous bag puts a little spring in your step on the way to work (and garners you a few compliments along the way), one thousand dollars is actually a reasonable price to pay. Hey, four dollars a day is the cost of a cappuccino in New York!

I've started to use style math not just at the point of buying a pricey item (yes, the sales staff at Henri Bendel and J. Crew love me now), but also when I examine the stuff sitting in my wardrobe that I had previously thought too good to wear. Every outing for the Diane von Furstenberg dress on which I was previously scared of spilling red wine now has increasing returns—the more I wear it, the more often I feel special and the less extortionate its price becomes.

Life really is too short to keep your best stuff for the best occasions. And also ponder this: the great stuff in life, the stuff that blindsides you with delight, often isn't the stuff you prepare and plan for. It's a random meeting with an old best friend, a smile from a stranger in a café, an impromptu night out with the girls from work, which leads to dinner, then karaoke, then an album of photos on Facebook, then bonding for life. So dress for today.

Even if nothing out of the ordinary happens to you that day, you've already made it better by unleashing your sexiest shoes/coat/blouse on an unsuspecting world.

DON'T JUST TAKE IT FROM ME . . .

"The first time I made money from my own business, when I was twenty-four, I bought myself a power suit. It cost me about one thousand dollars, and I wore the hell out of that suit. It fit beautifully and I looked like money walking down the street. I felt special every time I wore it. It doesn't fit me any-more, but I still keep it because it reminds me of a great time in my life."

Rosetta, 32, publisher, Gary, Indiana

"I'm not fully there yet—living for the moment, that is—but I'm trying because I deserve to. For the past five years I've been pregnant or nursing, and I feel now, *Enough already!* If I have something nice, I want to wear it and feel good. Despite my up-bringing being quite frugal and very much about not wearing your Sunday best except on Sundays, I know that clothes can make a woman feel good about herself—and that I owe it to myself to feel good every day."

Ann, 44, public-relations executive,
Goshen, Nova Scotia

IF YOU HAVE TO KEEP YOUR SUNDAY BEST FOR THE BEST . . .

Pay attention to your appearance. This doesn't involve huge amounts of money; it involves keeping the items you have clean, ironed, and stain free. And if you gain or lose weight, get new clothes that flatter your new shape.

25 Love Your Body

Women tend to zoom in on the one part of our bod-ies that we don't like and weave our whole body im-age into that one flawed zone. We become incapable of appreciating our shapely calves or long neck or healthy bosom if our bottom is too big or if our upper arms wobble a bit. It's as if we *want* to put ourselves down. It's not just about being fat, of course. Sometimes it's about being too thin or not toned enough.

This has to stop.

Love. Your. Body.

Please don't waste time under baggy shirts or cowering in the corner because you fear judgment. You are not as fat, thin, or wobbly as you think you are. And you know what? No one is even looking at you because we are too busy judging our own fat, thin, or wobbly bits.

For years, I dreamed of having a breast reduction. My mother and grandmother were flat chested—why had God or Mother Nature (I blamed both of them alternately) lumbered me with this pair of cumbersome watermelons? I tried everything to disguise them: wearing minimizer bras that didn't actually make them smaller but sort of flattened them and squidged the extra bits under my armpits, wearing men's rugby shirts with distracting stripes that performed—I thought at the time—a magic eye trick on people I was talking to, and even wearing turtleneck sweaters during the hottest months. Slouching was another trick. I was nearing six feet tall with a pair of gigantic knockers, so what wasn't to love about doubling over à la Quasimodo?

Finally, I got to the point where financially I could have afforded a boob job if I'd wanted one. But then a bright friend said, "But darling, your hooters balance out your bottom. At the moment, you're Monroe-esque.

Without those puppies, you'll just be a pancake on sturdy thighs!"

It was harsh but true. A lightbulb went on in my head. Rather than negatively focusing on one thing I hated, I started to look at the whole package. Yes, my boobs were not to my taste, but they did stop me from being pear shaped and kept me in the hourglass category.

Sometimes a farmer can't see the wood for the trees. Sometimes we women can't see the perfectly acceptable body shape for the minor imperfections we focus on.

DON'T JUST TAKE IT FROM ME . . .

"I have a daughter who is twenty-one and gorgeous, but she sees herself as something ugly. If I try to take her photo, she protests, says she looks awful, and rips up the photos when I get them developed. Every time this happens, I say to her, 'You'll look back on these times in five, ten, fifteen years, and you'll realize you were pretty darn good.' Young women need to see their beauty and not constantly compare themselves to the unattainable airbrushed images of celebrities."

Gina, 47, homemaker, Aberdeen, Scotland

"As we get older, I think feeling good in your skin is about health more than appearance. Your looks change, but your spirit and intellect make you sexy. It's not just the physical that should make you love yourself—it's the whole package."

Laurie, 43, writer, Boston

Go to a personal shopper or check out fashion magazines to see what styles suit your shape. It is all about using color, fabric, and cut to highlight your best bits. And if all else fails, wear black and carry an interesting pocketbook.

26 Splash Out on a Burberry Raincoat

A Burberry raincoat, or mackintosh ("mac"), as we call it in Burberry's birthplace, Great Britain, is a timeless classic. Audrey Hepburn, Jackie O., Madonna—what stylish star worth her sparkle has not wrapped up her frozen self in this famous bit of fabric when it's raining outside?

They are expensive, but if you take a roam around any old English country estate, you will see dames and ladies out doing the gardening in ones they've owned for more than fifty years. The coats last. And they never go out of style. When someone as fashion forward as Kate Moss can wear one with drainpipe jeans and a cigarette hanging out of her mouth and Hayden Panettierre can wear one elegantly over a dress to a charity event, you know this label has lost none of its appeal.

I'm a lazy fashionista. I want to look good, but I like things to be practical, too—so the idea of something hardy, weatherproof, and warm that still draws gasps of delight in a crowd is a win-win.

DON'T JUST TAKE IT FROM ME . . .

"The shape gives you a really classic silhouette and you can wear it with anything. It's flattering for every body shape, and the khaki color suits everyone—but if you're looking for a different shade, the brights will make you really stand out. The red will become a classic color in a Burberry mac soon."
Niria, 30, fashion director, New York City

"I go to lots of fashion weeks, and all the top editors wear it because the coat alone—even with jeans and flats—will make you look chic and polished. The main benefit of it is that it works for everyone, all year-round. It has a removable liner to give extra warmth when it's needed."
Marielle, 29, fashion editor, Brooklyn

IF YOU CAN'T SPLASH OUT ON A
BURBERRY RAINCOAT . . .

But you're still a fan of the legendary tartan print, go for the cheaper alternative: the umbrella. If you want the raincoat look, many good stores have imitated the design, so keep an eye out in department stores to acquire the same look for a lot less dough.

27 Buy Sexy Underwear

I'm not naturally sexy. As soon as I try to seduce someone or think about myself in a physical manner, I trip, wobble, and get my knicker elastic stuck on the bedpost. When it comes to being sexy, I need all the help I can get.

Sexy underwear, with the tiniest dangling of lace and undo-me-now ribbon, can turn the meekest cat into a sex kitten. It's worth the investment when you find yourself in a situation where a little bit of a fumble with a hot man may be in the cards and you need a boost. This is about you feeling sensuous and confident, luxurious and groomed, feminine and special. Treating yourself to gorgeous underwear and seeing how amazing you look in it is a simple way of reminding yourself of your value.

And as a bonus, any man would be lucky to see you in this lingerie. And any man would certainly think he'd died and gone to heaven to be able to remove this lingerie. If his tongue isn't hanging out and he's not trying to please you the first few times he sees you in nothing but your new undergarments, he's not worth the time. Because, honey, it's just going to get worse. In the bedroom, familiarity can breed a laissez-faire attitude to the whole compliment-'n'-foreplay package.

So what is sexy underwear? Am I telling you that

crotch-less panties and peephole bras are a good look? Er, no. They are about as erotic as a flasher in a park waving his pink worm about during daylight hours. No, sexy underwear is all about the glimpses, the softness, the surprises. You don't have to stick to black (although it is always a great fallback), but you shouldn't stick to red (it says prostitute if you go overboard). Sheer is always sexy, pinks are pretty, yellow is a nice surprise and looks great with a tan, lavender is delicate, purple is hot, color combos are daring and exotic, and bows on the derriere will suggest to your suitor that you're up for fun and games. More than anything, the men I've questioned on this topic are thrilled that you've made the effort. A sexy underwear set suggests this is a big deal for you. Grubby underwear says "whatever."

A few words of warning: don't do the full-on tassels, stockings, and garter belt getup the first time you get intimate. He'll either be intimidated or expect this level of lingerie performance every time you undress for him (I don't know which would be worse).

If you want to spoil him, spoil yourself first—it really is the perfect gift, which you'll both enjoy equally.

DON'T JUST TAKE IT FROM ME . . .

"I think it's important to make *you* feel sexy *before* the man—I want to differentiate between my grandma-underwear days and my sexy days. Men appreciate it because it shows you've made an effort."

Yael, 28, marriage and family therapist,
Calabasas, California

"My underwear is therapy—that's my treat. It's fun, it's different, and boyfriends do notice. People like different things so I spice it up a bit."

Stacey, 23, student, Fort Lauderdale, Florida

IF YOU CAN'T BUY SEXY NEW UNDERWEAR . . .

Look after the stuff you have. This is dull, ladies, but true: throwing your fancy bra and panties into the general wash will ruin them. Quickly. I've been stabbed in the rib cage by too many pieces of rogue underwire to ever do this again. Even if it means turning into a Biblical washerwoman on the weekends, buy some delicate detergent and gently scrub in your sink, then hang to dry naturally.

28 Learn to Pack Well

You'll all appreciate this feeling: You've just taken a long flight, you're feeling a bit soiled and stiff, and you need the restroom and the currency booth. The airport is dreary and the customs officials are stern and unwelcoming. *No matter,* you think—*I'll grab my suitcase and be on my way.* A vacation awaits, or at least, if you're traveling for business, a refreshing shower and a minibar! You stand at the baggage carousel. *Ping!* Finally your flight's cargo starts coming down the chute.

And yours never appears.

This happened to me once, on a tiny flight between Salvador and São Paulo in Brazil. I kept waiting and waiting, asking the stewards in very, very pigeon Portuguese if they could help me. After filling out a copious amount of forms (which both the authorities and I seemed to assume would be trashed the minute I left the security office), I left with nothing to wear and no real hope of ever seeing my case again.

In my MIA suitcase was a vintage T-shirt that I adored. It was an old Guns N' Roses tour shirt that a fashion designer friend of mine had slashed and altered and adorned with rainbow-colored diamanté. It sounds hideous, admittedly, but whenever I wore it, I seemed to have a great time, and there was not another one like it in existence in the world.

And that is when I decided to learn how to pack well.

Whenever at all possible, I pack a case small enough to carry on board with me. And at all other times, I don't pack anything that I would be broken-hearted to lose. My traveler's life has become much more simple.

For the first year after losing my bag, on my return from every holiday—beach, skiing, adventure, city break, etc.—I would make a note of exactly what I wore, what I tried on but hated, and what never left my suitcase. After a few trips I soon learned that I don't need to take two anoraks and three sweaters— one sweater and an umbrella will suffice. My hair looks like a mess on the beach whatever I do, so I don't need to pack my hair dryer and other appliances, just a hair band to keep it swept back in a ponytail. And however much I want to be a *bella signora* on a city break, it is never gonna happen. I could take and apply the whole beauty department of Macy's, but it is going to slide off my face after a few hours of walking and climbing, so why bother? And as for jewelry and high heels . . . please! On vacation, less is certainly more. The jewelry would live in the hotel-room safe and the heels would be dismissed for flip-flops.

Some people travel with a full-on medicine cabinet. This is a bit overcautious, as most hotels and places of lodging will be able to take care of any emergency. But of course your prescriptions, a few headache pills, and stomach-upset medicine are always good to have and barely take up any room at all. Keep anything that can leak separate, and double protect yourself by placing it all in a secure, liquid-proof plastic bag.

Be organized. Ring ahead to the place you're staying to find out what amenities they have. If you're going somewhere a bit strange, ask them for a packing-essentials list (I'm all about lists!) to give you guidelines that are easy to follow. When I went to Mexico recently, I asked for a list and was surprised to see a flashlight on there—but when I showed up and realized there was no electricity at the retreat after eight o'clock in the evening, I was glad I thought to ask.

So pack with precision. Make useful lists. It will save you time, laundry, and backache as you're lugging your stuff. And try not to take anything that you couldn't bear never to see again, but if you must, keep it on you at all times.

DON'T JUST TAKE IT FROM ME . . .

"The first time I went traveling to Europe, I packed a huge bag. Crossing the English Channel, I was so fed up with lugging it around, I almost chucked it in! Now I lay everything out on the bed a few days before I travel and analyze what I actually need. I then halve it. You do not need as much as you think you do. Wherever you're heading, take a black skirt, a black pair of pants, and lots of different colored tops that you can mix and match."

Dalia, 39, translator, Beijing

"Anything you can't carry yourself, you shouldn't be bringing—that's my rule. A good bag is important. Get wheels! It'll save your back. I used to take a pharmacy-load of stuff with me on vacation, but I learned to rely on toiletries from the hotel. If stuff you need isn't there, ask the hotel staff, who are usually helpful. Or buy it in the country you're in—it's fun to try new things."

Nicole, 30, restaurant manager,
Santa Fe, New Mexico

IF YOU CAN'T LEARN TO PACK WELL . . .

Learn to unpack well. Yes, it's boring when a cocktail by the hotel pool at sunset awaits, but take five minutes to hang up your key items—in the bathroom, where the steam can uncrease the wrinkles if possible.

29 Get Professionally Fitted for a Bra

The wrong bra–wearing lady is an easy-to-spot breed, and sadly, she's more common than a monkey in the Peruvian rain forest.

Her habitat: everywhere, except the changing room of a respected lingerie store.

Her markings: a hump, red strap marks, and boobs that resemble bowls of Jell-O on a washing machine (or perhaps she has four boobs instead of two—greedy, miss!).

I was in denial about my ample chest for the longest time. I foolishly wandered around in strange white cotton trainer bras for many years before upgrading to the largest size I deemed just the right side of mortification: 34DD.

Fresh from the shower, at the beginning of the day, my breasts would behave quite nicely. They'd snuggle into their cotton cups and proudly produce a flattering cleavage. But a few moves later—and certainly after a light jog for the bus—they'd be here, there, and everywhere. I'd constantly have to rearrange my pair in the restroom or surreptitiously under a coat. I looked as though I was all about self-loving, but really it was a bit of self-loathing.

Then a good friend told me that not only do ill-fitting bras actually make your bosom appear bigger, but a poor fit increases the speed of the sag factor because the bra can't do what it was paid to do: support you!

I took myself to the Queen of Tit-iana, Rigby & Peller, the underapparel merchant to the Queen of England, no less. Ushered behind a red velvet curtain, my useless item was tossed to the side as a strict German lady with a good pair of eyes, lots of experience, and a measuring tape fiddled, thrusted, and manhandled me. I came out more than a hundred pounds poorer and a 29F. Now, is that an impressive bra size or what?

It used to be a struggle to find the right size if you didn't fall into the average range, but unusual-size lingerie is cropping up all over the Internet now, at reasonable prices and in sexy styles. You can even buy bikini separates that allow for an ample cleavage and blouses specially invented not to burst at the buttons under the pressure of your décolletage. Boobs can stop being a handicap and start being an asset when placed in the right hands—oops, I mean cups!

Investigate. Get yourself measured. Throw away the bad bras that leave red blotches, backaches, and bulges, and you won't be tripping over your nipples in a few years' time.

DON'T JUST TAKE IT FROM ME . . .

"You have to go, even though it's embarrassing. Yes, you get groped and pummeled by an old lady, but it pays off. Go to a nice place—a department store is the best place. Afterward clothes fit you better and weight is taken off your back. It's a free boob job and you look thinner. The uncomfortable digging-in stops and the red marks vanish."

Rachel, 28, writer, West Hartford, Connecticut

"It wasn't the cup that was wrong for me, but the back width. I worked at Victoria's Secret while I was in college in upstate New York, and I was wearing a 34C. A perk—excuse the pun—of the job was getting a fitting, and it turned out I was a 36B. My boobs looked so much better. Being properly sized suited me better, and clothes looked better on me."

Stacey, 25, banking assistant, Buffalo, New York

Learn how to do it yourself. And remember that you don't stay the same size forever—you'll fluctuate with weight and the time of the month—so keep measuring regularly. Get yourself a measuring tape with inches on it. Measure just beneath your boobs, around your rib cage. This is your numerical back size. Then measure around the fullest part of your breasts. Every extra inch more than your back size is an extra letter in cup size. So one inch more than your back size is an A cup, two inches more is a B, and so on.

30 Learn to Walk in Three-Inch Stilettos

High heels are enduringly seductive, but when it comes to walking in them, it's tempting to say "forget it." Many women stick to sensible ballet pumps and sneakers, and it's easy to see why—you get everywhere quicker, for one thing. But I'm starting to think we're in a bit too much of a rush. Tottering about a few inches higher than God intended forces us to slow down, put grace before speed, and develop a sexy wiggle.

Marilyn Monroe was a big advocate of stilettos. She famously sawed a tiny bit off one shoe in each pair to exaggerate her swinging hips and plump derriere. I haven't gone that far yet, but finally at the age of thirty I did a Nicole Kidman: I embraced my height and went shopping for my own pair of skyscrapers.

Not only do you gain extra height with heels, which my research of real women shows anyone under five foot eight desperately wants, but wearing them changes your whole posture. Slip on a pair and you instantly stand up straighter without the help of an uncomfortable corset, your bottom sticks out seductively, your legs look longer (especially if you wear pants or hosiery in the same color as the shoes), and your shoulders drop back. Sexy!

Three-inch stilettos are not for the drunk, the blister prone, or the sprinters among us. But the rest of us should all just understand that sometimes looking beautiful can be a burden. The saying "no pain, no gain" has never been more true than after three hours of dancing in heels. Accept the pain, and enjoy how beautifully you glide ever onward.

DON'T JUST TAKE IT FROM ME . . .

"When you stand in a group of ten-year-olds and they tower over you, stilettos become your life. How to wear them? You can't stand in one spot for too long, so keep moving. Call your fabulous gay friends who've done drag for tips. They bark at me at parties if I take the heels off because my feet swell and I'll never get the heels back on again. You should shop for these shoes at night and always buy them a bit bigger. Heels tap into your sexy power and make you walk differently."

Delaina, 33, writer, Suffern, New York

"I have to wear heels all the time, and I wear them down to the ground and then get them reheeled. The pain thing is all mind over matter. Wearing heels makes you look taller and thinner and the angle makes you sexy, so they're worth the blisters. Men notice you. It's weird—maybe it's a confident air you give out. Men stare, especially at a skirt and heels combo. It's fabulously sexy."

Laura, 27, reporter, Tiverton, Nova Scotia

IF YOU CAN'T LEARN TO WALK IN THREE-INCH STILETTOS . . .

Go high in an easier manner. Platforms and wedges don't have the same dramatic effect, but they have come a long way since the seventies. If you've got short legs or cankles (ankles as thick as your calves), avoid the ones with ribbon ties at all costs.

31 Find the Perfect Pair of Jeans

Wearing the right pair of jeans for your body shape means the difference between looking like a hot mama and a lumpy pile of lard. Never, ever purchase jeans without trying them on. And don't settle on the first pair—grab every single style and shade in the store and lock yourself in a cubicle for as long as you need. Once you find a pair that you know looks good (you know when you're settling for something that's not quite right), buy a few pairs. These pesky companies do tend to discontinue denim styles just when you've discovered your personal jean Holy Grail.

I didn't have a clue about jeans—and what they could do for your bottom—for quite some years. I had a misspent youth wearing Levi's 501s, the sexiest thing a man's bottom can ever be encased in but not so alluring on a girl. It didn't occur to me I should stop trying to look like my favorite male pop stars and actually take a backward glance in the mirror. If I had, I would have seen that I looked as if I were wearing balloon pants.

Thankfully, with the advent of the boot-cut style, I was saved. Tight in my biggest area and flaring out to give balance at the knee, the pants suddenly gave me a shape. It looked as though I'd dropped two dress sizes in the changing room. My boy-style bottoms were committed to the local charity shop, and I went in search of the style (not necessarily the label) that suited me most.

There are all sorts of jeans—find yours.

Skinny jeans are fabulous for the thin (shockingly unflattering on the heavyset, I've accepted with a tear in my eye).

Full-on flares, matched with a fitted top, are great for the curvier among us but should be avoided like the plague by the more diminutive girl.

Boot-cut jeans are good for most bodies, particularly the pear shaped.

Low-rise jeans appear to be sexy—until you bend over, and suddenly the world is invited to judge your taste in panties.

High-waisted jeans make even the most flat-stomached lady appear to be in

the second trimester of pregnancy
and therefore should be worn with
great precaution and certainly not on
bloated days (or if you're planning on
a big plate of nachos and a few
margaritas that evening).

We all have different-size waists, bottoms, and legs,
but the perfect pair is out there for you, I promise. Too
many women feel that they have to consign jeans to
their teen years or treat them like tracksuit bottoms—
practical but pretty shapeless.

Fight the fear. The right pair can take you from day
to night in the most casually sexy way with the addition of high heels and a pair of earrings.

Just always look behind you as you leave the fitting
room.

DON'T JUST TAKE IT FROM ME . . .

"There's always a way to wear leggings or skinny jeans, but it
needs to be appropriate. Usually with boots and a long dress.
Camel toe is nasty. Sausage legs are hideous. The clue's in the
title—if you've got chubby legs, don't do skinny jeans."

Sonia, 28, finance officer, San Diego, California

"Go somewhere where there are hundreds of pairs to try on,
and grab a male shop assistant and ask his opinion—not a
woman's—because he'll tell you which one makes your ass look
hot. I've learned that boot cut is the best. They sit on the hip.
It's essential that you don't show crack, and remember, belts
can give you a muffin-top issue."

Jen, 25, flight attendant, Charlotte, North Carolina

NO REGRETS

Find another casual clothing item that you know rocks your shape. A classic cotton T-shirt that works well with anything is a must. If you have great arms, show them off with a cap sleeve. If you don't like your arms, get a shirt with sleeves that finish at the elbow for a flattering look. If you have a big chest, go for a V-neck. If you have a bony décolletage, go for a high-cut scoop neck. Thick around the middle? Don't cheat your size. Go loose rather than tight with the fit of your clothes.

32 Show Off Your Legs

Strut your stuff, ladies. I'm not suggesting you wear a "fanny skimmer," as my Great-Great-Auntie Joyce so eloquently puts it, just something grazing the top of the knee that flatters and flaunts in equal measure.

I remember being mortified when I got my first glimpse of the dreaded orange peel when I was twenty years old. At that point I declared to be a trouser gal, and I covered up studiously. But I realized we all have flaws and no one is perfect; even supermodels look so glorious only after a good oiling-up and the right lighting. Just ask their surgeons. If you're up for uncovering, follow these simple rules:

Get a tan (fake is fantastic) because pasty pins can verge on being puttylike, however slim.

Exfoliate, shave, and moisturize.

Train your knees to sit together like a lady's (after years of wearing blush-sparing pants, I really had to train myself to remember this simple act of discretion).

Wear panties. The world may be ready for your unleashed legs, but it is not ready to see what is between them.

Learn how to pose in photos: put your legs together, turn to one side, and lean slightly forward, thereby diminishing any thunder-thigh anxiety. Never allow yourself to be snapped from below. If you have cellulite worries, place your hands over any particular regions a camera may pick up on (this is so easily done, I'm now happy posing in a bikini).

Legs shouldn't be out after Labor Day or before Easter, except on vacations in hot places.

Walk tall and enjoy your body.

DON'T JUST TAKE IT FROM ME . . .

"I follow a simple rule to avoid looking too much like a tart: choose legs or cleavage; don't show off everything in one go. Either one or the other is enough to ignite the interest of the guys around you. Both and you go from being a girl they want to date to a girl they just want to sleep with."

Clara, 35, legal secretary, Sandusky, Ohio

"Keeping your legs groomed and orderly gives you the confidence to show them off. We all have flaws, but we should all be confident to get our legs out—as long as there's not something too awful that could put your friends off their breakfast. Learn how to flash just the right amount—may it be an ankle, to the knee, or a full-on 'here I come' hot-pants moment."

Sheena, 39, marketing manager, London

IF YOU CAN'T SHOW OFF YOUR LEGS . . .

Show off another feature you love. We aren't all blessed with perfect pins. My mother has been plagued by varicose veins and is very self-conscious of her appearance from the waist down. Luckily for my adorable mum, she has a beautiful face and an elegant neck, which she always emphasizes with carefully chosen jewelry. Find your own bit you're proud to show off!

33 Get Comfy in Uggs

Oh yes, they are ugly, but for the love of all things wonderful, just slip on a pair and reevaluate your stance on these sheepskin boots.

I fought this losing battle for ten years—and why? The minute I gave in, during a particularly chilly March in New York City, I saw stars. My hardened, stressed commuter feet rejoiced as if suddenly bathed in soft clouds. Wearing Uggs felt better than having a massage at the best spa in Manhattan.

I only wish I hadn't been so snooty before and that I'd slipped them onto my poor cold trotters the minute I left university at twenty-one years old.

Now they come everywhere with me. Wearing Uggs makes any place feel like home—suddenly a hellish plane journey feels acceptable or a wander round to the store for groceries doable.

The only problem is that they are so comfy, you might feel as though you already have your slippers on and happily stomp dirt around your home before realizing your mistake. I have even been known to sleep in them. A friend has had to sort me out by buying me the slipper variety for Christmas.

Friends still think I'm a bit naff, but hey, what do they know. If they just slipped a few toes into the fluffy warmth, they'd know what I was going on about. I am well aware that I look like an Australian sheep farmer. But I don't care and my feet certainly don't either.

DON'T JUST TAKE IT FROM ME . . .

"I have a pair in every color. They are so ugly but amazing. Just get them, get them now. They are the comfiest shoes. And pay the money for the real ones—the fake ones don't count. I wish I'd worn them since I was born. Now they have wedge ones, so even if you're short and want extra height, you can do them."

Shauna, 26, writer, Malibu, California

"I got them only because they were on Oprah's Christmas wish list and I trust whatever Oprah says. Before that, I was quite a snob. I still look down and see Frankenstein's monster's feet when I'm wearing them because I'm shoe size nine and a half. So I don't wear them to be cute, but they're the best thing ever to commute in."

Katie, 28, editor, Atlanta

IF YOU CAN'T GET COMFY IN UGGS . . .

At least remember to pack flat shoes when you're out and about in heels. A few hours and a few inches up plays havoc with your toes—and your back. So my trick is to keep some comfy flip-flops and ballet slippers for smart occasions where my Uggs would be too bad but my heels would be just too uncomfortable to endure the whole evening.

34 Spanx It Up

These pants have saved my life on many occasions. Yes, they're as restricting as a wet suit and as uncomfortable as Velcroing your pubic hair to a fast-moving truck, but by golly, they work. They turn a wobbly bottom into buns of steel. With these elasticized panties holding down your chubby bits, that slightly-too-tight dress becomes flatteringly skimming again. Those trousers in which you were scared to sit down are suddenly formfitting and sexy.

Spanx—or the invention sent from heaven, as I like to think of them—give you confidence and a smoother shape. So what if they take you thirty minutes to prize over your bottom half? Who cares if you cannot physically go to the loo the whole time you're wearing them? You can drop a dress size without two weeks of cardio at six in the morning.

My Spanx officially became my undercover hero earlier this year. Picture it: me, a curvy size ten, judging skinny and excitable bikini-clad teens for Miss America 2008. What an honor it was to be asked. Growing up in England, I'd always envied you marvelous Yanks and your pageants and proms and all-around celebration of glamour. The other judges and I had been in Vegas for a week, being force-fed five-course meals by Nevada's most fabulous billionaires and downing champagne. The bloat! The horrific bloat! As I sat ticking boxes and watching these gym bunnies strut back and forth, I needed a quick fix before the live televised finale and I knew twenty-four hours in the gym and a colonic weren't the answer.

Spanx to the rescue!

The big night arrived, and with an inelegant struggle and a fair bit of wiggling, my muffin tops were encased and my bloated tummy had deflated (even if artificially under the ironlike strength of my knickers). Where had my extra bits gone? Who knew! They were MIA and I felt fine. Yes, I was still a curvy size ten judging girls ten years younger than me and half my size. But with the big panties holding me in, I knew I could hold my own.

DON'T JUST TAKE IT FROM ME . . .

"I just tried them on for the first time, and first I was like, 'I can't breathe.' Then I was like, 'My ass looks fantastic.' No ripples.

NO REGRETS

You feel slinkier instantly. They take away love handles and give you an hourglass shape. You have to get used to them and I wouldn't wear them to work, but for an evening out and when you're feeling bloated—perfect!"

Karen, 26, health editor, Queens, New York

"We all have fat days. Even if we're not physically fatter, we feel it and that affects our mood, our confidence, our need to throw staplers at the heads of our colleagues. I control these angry, miserable days by piling my butt into my big, tight knickers. My ass looks less like two rhinos having a face-off when it's in these!"

Julie, 35, office manager, Telluride, Colorado

IF YOU CAN'T SPANX IT UP . . .

Try tight-grip stockings. The darker the shade, the more slimming they look. And just that extra support from wearing control-top hosiery will make you feel better.

35 Buy a Princess Dress

Every girl wants to grow up to be a princess. Not for the big castle, the charming prince, or the stable of horses. No, little girls are after the wardrobe. The flowing robes encrusted with jewels, made from the finest silks or satins, showing just enough décolletage to be alluring without revealing too much. Hey, what's not to love about looking fabulous, sexy, and classy all at the same time?

As we get older, princess fantasies give way to budget restraints and practicality. It becomes cooler to wear jeans or to prove your worth in a power suit. In our modern, grown-up struggle, some femininity and delicacy can get lost.

But they shouldn't. Don't wait for your wedding day to wear a dress in which you feel delicious, and after that day don't think you'll never look like a duchess of style again. You work hard, you love hard, you play hard—buy a floaty frock, even if it's just for fun. I'm lucky—a friend with connections snagged me a discount on the dress of my dreams, and it's the best thing I ever purchased. Black and strapless, it hits the floor in a chiffon swirl while my bust twinkles with delicate gems. It's a Marchesa and it is too, too fabulous. Not only does it make me feel good when I'm wearing it, it makes me feel good just knowing it's hanging up in my closet.

The ubiquitous LBD (little black dress) is a staple of any girl's wardrobe, of course, but it's more of a handy must-have to fall back on than the stuff dreams are made of.

Buy yourself one princess dress and make excuses to wear it: stay in fabulous hotels, attend glittering balls, accept invitations to black-tie weddings, enter competitions to get yourself a seat at an awards show. Anywhere fabulous deserves a fabulous dress. And yes, royalty doesn't come cheap. But if the dress is classic, beautifully made, and suited to your shape, you can wear it forever. And each time you do, I swear, you'll feel more beautiful and younger than before.

DON'T JUST TAKE IT FROM ME . . .

"Every woman should have a princess dress in her wardrobe! Call it the Cinderella syndrome. We all need to own a belle-of-the-ball gown, with a little too much tulle that cries for a tiara, though we wouldn't be caught dead in one. We need to be able to live the fairy tale, even if the horse and carriage is just a taxi."

Susannah, 34, fashion editor, New York City

"I have this divine corseted number that I bought four years ago (and am still paying for). It was expensive but I had to have it. It's boned and structured so well that the minute it's zipped up, my ample bosoms become playful and pert and my waist is cinched in to the point of being childlike. I can't tell you the number of times I've been asked out while wearing it. Even now, I'm married but still love to feel men's eyes graze me appreciatively as I sashay into a party."

Katie, 31, restaurant hostess, Washington, DC

IF YOU CAN'T BUY A PRINCESS DRESS . . .

Invest in some fabulous costume jewelry. A gorgeous choker or a collection of stunning bangles will dress up the aforementioned LBD and become a talking point. Look for deep jewel-like colors (reds, greens, blues) and fake it with pride—no one can tell the real value of a piece of jewelry nowadays, anyway.

WILDERNESS WOMAN

36 Kayak on a Phosphorus Lake at Midnight

Now, until you've done this, you don't realize what you've been missing, but you just have to jump into a kayak and go for it.

Kayaking, at midnight or otherwise, had never been part of my life.

Then I heard about a lake in Puerto Rico, in the middle of nowhere, a few hours inland from the old city of San Juan. It apparently glowed. And anything that went into it, on it, or through it caused a cascade of fluorescence so beautiful, you couldn't believe your eyes. As soon as I'd heard about it once, I kept hearing about it. Suddenly everyone I knew had been there or to one like it in Jamaica or Belize. Everyone described it as something everyone should witness to understand nature at its most amazing. Clearly the universe was telling me I was supposed to try it out.

So a friend and I checked into a hotel in Puerto Rico and rushed down to get supplies in a local shop: soccer-style shorts, bikinis, and bottles of water—and yes, jelly shoes.

After an endless journey through the forest with our guide, we emerged at the side of a lake surrounded by mangroves. Jumping into our waiting kayaks, we paddled silently under the moon.

When we emerged into an open pool, everything came alive. This was the phosphorous lake—and suddenly our oars' splashes turned to liquid silver. Any movement sparked a glorious reaction. Bright bubbles of light burst and darted around, like tropical fish fleeing from tourists. We got braver and started running our hands and feet through the water.

We rowed back to the edge of the lake, tired and damp and desperate for room service, yet so privileged to have seen one of the wonders of the world untouched by man.

DON'T JUST TAKE IT FROM ME . . .

"It sounds like a chore, I know, exercising at night, far away from all your creature comforts, to see things that glow. But it's worth it because you can't explain it. And let's be honest, we are rarely excited or speechless anymore."

Cassie, 30, cinema administrator, New York City

"As a child, I had trouble sleeping, so my father stuck these glow-in-the-dark stars and moons onto the ceiling above my bed. From the first night I saw them, I adored them. I picked them off and stuck them back on again every time we moved— even when I moved into my college dorm. Hearing about a real-life nighttime fluorescent fest was something I had to see with my own eyes, and it was beautiful."

Janice, 26, trainer, Lincoln, Nebraska

IF YOU CAN'T KAYAK ON A PHOSPHOROUS LAKE AT MIDNIGHT . . .

Try kayaking in daylight on crystal blue waters. It's easier to arrange and perhaps a little less scary. Just remember: however far you go out, you have to get back again, so save your strength.

37 Take On a Physical Challenge

Are you a lazybones? I am! I'd love to be one of those people who jumps out of bed at six in the morning to run to the gym. But I'm not. I'm more of a—how can I say it?—"Really? The gym? Really?" kind of girl. It's the whole overheatin' 'n' sweatin' business. Yuck. I'd much prefer at any point to be sitting under a tree in the shade with a good book and a glass of pinot grigio.

But as my personal trainer reminds me whenever I actually make an appointment, "Your ass ain't gonna get any goddamn smaller sitting under no tree—and wine is a waste of calories. Move it."

The problem I've found is staying motivated. What's to love about a gray air-conditioned gym filled with grunting men in too-short shorts? Zilch. The words *elliptical trainer* make me yawn. Treadmills give me narcolepsy. And as for rowing machines, yes, I know they work every muscle in your body, but please, they must be the devil's work themselves.

That's how the gym feels to me.

That's why I think I must have been feeling particularly unhealthy—or had a lobotomy—the day I signed up to do a bikini boot camp. It was cold and gray outside; I was chubby and zapped of energy. This camp on a beach in Mexico seemed to be the answer. I skimmed past the details of six a.m. starts and beach runs to the page about sunset yoga and hibiscus tea mocktail hour. This was just what I needed.

Looking at the chalkboard of the day's activities on the first morning (yes, at six o'clock in the morning) nearly sent me into a complete body breakdown. I wouldn't be able to cope. Yes, there were women twice my age enrolled, too, but they had a kind of twinkle in their eye that implied they could handle anything. Even the roly-poly girl who I thought would be my partner in skipping-class crime was dressed head to toe in Lycra and karate kicking next to the hammocks. Bugger. What had I done?

Then something bizarre happened. I was so busy rubbernecking at the other fabulous people, admiring the view of the sea, feeling the sun on my back, and struggling to keep up that before I knew it I was completing two-hour circuit classes with a smile on my face. Or finishing up a yoga class so energized that I'd actually volunteer to go on an hour-long power walk along the shore afterward.

This is when it hit me: taking your workout outside makes you feel alive, rather than feeling like a rat in a laboratory. Suddenly, those runners who'd pass me on the way to the deli on Sunday mornings made sense. Moving your workout into the real world somehow makes it more vital.

By the end of the week, not only was I able to cycle for fourteen miles happily, the trip went down as one of the most purely happy times of my life. Doing yourself good—mentally and physically—is a great thing. I caught myself at one point cycling along, waving to the locals, and singing "Someone Saved My Life Tonight" by Elton John with great gusto and abandon.

Think more creatively about working out. If the idea of going to a gym fills you with great dread, be inventive and just get moving! You don't have to hate it for it to work. Power walk your neighborhood. Hike. Swim. Get a bike and ride. Join a soccer league.

Be safe and enjoy. It's amazing the calories you can burn when you've not got a timer ticking away.

DON'T JUST TAKE IT FROM ME . . .

"Solo bike rides in the park after work soon turned into private practice sessions for riding with no hands. I set myself a challenge and it kept me working out. With no time limit and no one to laugh when I crashed into stuff, it was the ideal time to get fit."

Eloise, 30, writer, New York City

"As a horse-mad teen, I desperately wanted to be a cowgirl. A ranch-hand vacation with my best friend after university realized my dream and I spent weeks outdoors, riding and getting fresh air. I moved back to an office job in the city shortly afterward, but I loved the wrangling experience so much that it's still my secret plan B."

Jane, 29, accountant, Hoboken, New Jersey

At least make exercise interesting. Yes, running on a treadmill is time efficient, but you will lose motivation quickly. Sign up to take a martial-arts or dance class. Pair up with a friend to attend local step or spinning classes. Buy yourself a smart workout outfit and new sneakers so you feel good exercising. And don't feel discouraged if you fall off the keep-fit wagon for a few days (or weeks). Just learn to tell the difference between being lazy and being genuinely tired and run-down.

38 Let Go of the Edge of an Ice Rink

As we get older, everything becomes scarier. Is it because we feel we have more to lose if something goes wrong? Or is it simply that all our fears stem from a fear of dying and as we grow older the reality of death becomes clearer? It's amazing the harness that fear can put on our ability to take risks and have fun. Sometimes we need to test ourselves and embrace our inner child just to know that life without risk and daring is nothing.

A symbolically simple way of seeing this is to take yourself to an ice rink. As a child, I'm sure you begged to go skating every time winter came around. As an adult, not so much. As a child, you'd whiz around, rosy cheeked and giggling with your pals. You'd heard rumors of the girl in the class above who got her finger sliced off, but you also watched the Olympics and dreamed of one day scoring a perfect ten while dressed in a cerise sequined number. Skating wasn't scary, it was fun.

Revisit a rink now. It's frightening. You get the show-offs, who are determined to perfect their triple axels regardless of blundering people behind them. Then you get the cocky teenage stewards who are supposedly there to keep order but are really interested only in flirting with girls while skating backwards. Where do you fit?

I went skating as an adult for the first time a couple of years ago at Rockefeller Center with some weekend visitors. After stopping in at the adjacent bar for a few fortifying glasses of wine, we hit the rink like nervous tortoises. We clutched the side, getting in the way of the more dynamic three-year-olds whizzing past.

Then, after a few circuits, it got boring. So I thought, what's the worst that can happen? No one ever died on an ice rink (I don't think). I could lose a finger, but it's highly unlikely, and I can just keep my fingers curled under if I fall. A bruised bottom would be a badge of honor—that didn't bother me. Aching muscles? Hey, it shows I've had a much-needed workout.

So off we went, a bit pathetically, but at least we were off, and it was fun to get some momentum and feel the air rushing past us. My friends and I held hands, got a rhythm going to the random nineties dance tunes blasting out over the speakers, and laughed. This was such innocent fun. Who knew you could have this much fun with your clothes on?

It doesn't have to be ice skating. Snowboarding and waterskiing are great options as well. Any risk will spice up your life. But I look at letting go of the edge of an ice rink as a metaphor for life. Pushing yourself out onto the slippery surface is tricky, it gives your muscles a bit of a workout, and you might look silly for a bit, but everyone has gloriously rosy cheeks and huge grins at the end of it.

DON'T JUST TAKE IT FROM ME . . .

"Ice skating is nothing to me anymore! Traveling alone through New Zealand after university, I decided to test my courage to the limit by doing a solo bungee jump. Hurling myself headfirst off the 141-foot Kawarau Bridge was ten times harder than anything I'd ever done before, and halfway down I wished I'd been strapped to the tasty instructor. But it was a great feeling when it was over. And the best bit? Having no one around to talk me out of it."

Louise, 30, photo researcher, London

"I've tried to remove the word *can't* from my vocabulary. At least until I've tried something once or know that pursuing a particular line of adventure could lead to my certain death. Since opening up like this, I've had so much more fun. Ice skating when it's cold outside, jumping off a thirty-foot cliff into the sea in the summertime. Once you do something fun and don't kill yourself, it pushes you on to live life with a reckless abandon."

Rose, 33, financial investor, London

IF YOU CAN'T LET GO OF THE EDGE OF AN ICE RINK . . .

Pursue another activity you loved as a child. Join an adult soccer league, or take your nephews out to a water park. We spend so much time being serious grown-ups; it can be freeing and stress relieving to regress sometimes.

39 Go Camping

I'm not going to lie to you—I'm a Ritz Carlton kind of a gal! I like Frette sheets, Acqua di Parma bubble bath, and a concierge who books my restaurants. But I'm also up for adventure, fresh air, enjoying nature, and having a few weekends away that don't break the bank.

My earliest memories of camp aren't the happiest. In London, all Girl Guides were sent to a particular camp for one weekend per year—it was famous for being pretty, with lots of good walks and a well-stocked sweetshop. The problem for me was that it was in my village. While girls from other parts of London got onto a bus and escaped their parents for a few days, I walked round and would bump into my mum on forest walks. How rubbish is that?

The other major downer was that I was always stuck with a whining girl called Katie, who had somehow got away with telling the Guide leaders that she was allergic to dish detergent. So, yes, you guessed it, muggins here would be stuck doing double duty while Katie looked on, telling me if I'd missed a bit.

But camping has got sexier, and when you're an adult, lots of new things open up. Choose a field where you're allowed to take your car as close to the campsite as possible, so you're not lugging stuff on your back for days. I also recommend heading somewhere with a shop nearby so if you're really craving a pizza or tub of ice cream after living on nuts and berries for two days, you can treat yourself.

And you'll have to decide whether you want to go with worthy campers or happy campers. Worthy campers think you should live like cavemen: they don't believe in cutting corners or cheating nature, so you exist on fires, plastic sheets, and a backpack's worth of tinned food, which has to be rationed out daily. Forget board games or booze—any extra backpack space is given over to a medical kit and a Swiss army knife.

A happy camper, on the other hand, knows that a liquor store and barbecue dinner are only thirty minutes away and can be patronized at any point in the trip. A happy camper knows that although protein bars have their purpose, Ferrero Rocher chocolates are much more delicious. A happy camper has also checked out the washing facilities in advance and knows that if, by day two, there is still no hot water, rather than "grinning and bearing it" à la a worthy camper, she is making her happy way to the nearest guesthouse—or back home, via Pizza Hut.

DON'T JUST TAKE IT FROM ME . . .

"My whole family thinks I'm prissy, but I go camping all the time. I like to sleep in a tent—even though it's kind of scary. At the Boonville Beer Festival in northern California, my fiancé and I go, drink, and pass out in our crappy tent. It's fun. Camp food is great—even though you're eating bad stuff like hot dogs and marshmallows and more beer, you feel healthy just because you're out in the fresh air."

Shelby, 29, speech therapist, Boise, Idaho

"I love camping because it's the one holiday I have where I can live in my own dirt and forget about wearing makeup or ironing my clothes. I love that the focus is taken off the external and put onto the internal."

Delia, 31, potter, Charleston, West Virginia

IF YOU CAN'T GO CAMPING . . .

Don't beat yourself up about it. It is more fun than it sounds, I promise, but if you really can't be dragged away from your luxurious hotel, perhaps try the middle ground instead: a hut on a beach, with a no-shoes, no-news rule. This will feel more nature oriented and less like home, and if you're lucky, they might have a wireless connection and flushing toilets.

40 Appreciate Each Changing Season

People can go from bed to car to office to gym to a crowded bar to bed without ever looking up to see the sun. What a waste. Living your life under artificial lighting is a shame. Remember how as a child each season seemed to last forever? How each time the season changed you'd be in shock at how different the small world you owned looked? The changing weather meant a change of pursuits, bedtimes, and outfits, and it kept life exciting. Try to get that feeling back by appreciating the changing seasons. It's good for your soul.

Here are a few things to look for in each season:

Spring: chocolate eggs, the smell of green grass, the return of bright sunlight through your blinds in the morning, peonies, damp forests, April showers, public holidays, risking a trip to the shore, family Easters, the sudden urge to get fit, the sudden urge to clean your house, March Madness sales, new beginnings, bunny rabbits, birdsongs, blossoms.

Summer: sun-bleached hair, salty air, leaving the office early on Fridays, ice-cream sundaes, all-night deck parties, warm breezes, lighter traffic, mojitos, boat trips, baseball, hot dogs, Fourth of July fireworks, your boss going away for a week on vacation and leaving you alone, you going away for a week on vacation and turning off your phone, flip-flops, miniature golf, roller coasters, water guns, drinking homemade lemonade on a porch, freckles, snoozing in the shade, white linen in beach houses, sangria.

Autumn: crunching through fallen brown leaves, pumpkins lit on stoops, having an excuse to bake cakes rather than go out, turkey and all the trimmings, nestling down with your family, rewatching old horror movies, trick-or-treating, eating chicken wings and ribs while cheering during a football game, digging out your old sweaters, watching the days get shorter and shorter, surviving on soup and fresh bread and butter, knowing you can eat too much candy happily because you're not going to have to show off your tummy in a bikini for a good few months.

Winter: hibernating under comforters, the smell of cinnamon and oranges, warming frozen bottoms with a real log fire, receiving more mail in the post, finding the perfect gifts for your favorite people, doing impressions from *A Christmas Story,* baking shortbread, drinking eggnog and Baileys (separately or together), sleeping in thermal pajamas and toasty socks, seeing your boss tipsy at the office party, ringing in the New Year and deciding how to improve your life, anxiously awaiting the postman and florist on Valentine's Day, making snow angels, having unshaven legs, walking warily on icy pavements that look as if they've been coated with sparkle, wearing glitter to parties, dragging a fir tree home, getting the perfect gift.

DON'T JUST TAKE IT FROM ME . . .

"I'm a summer baby. I always loved the warmer months, and the rest were just a drag to get through before it was summer again. But as I've gotten older and time is speeding up and away from me, I've really learned to appreciate each day, and season, as it comes. I have a tree outside my house, and each morning as I'm getting ready for the day I take a second to look at it. Sometimes it's bare, sometimes it provides a home for tweeting birds protecting their offspring, and sometimes it's bursting with color."

Ina, 41, real-estate agent, Philadelphia

"The seasons, to me, represent four chances per year to get your life back on track. Everyone has her New Year's resolutions, but after a few weeks, if we cheat or fail, we feel that's it for the year. That's not the case. Look at the year as four segments, each with a different energy and priority—and each handing you a fresh start. For example, don't just think that summer is the time you need to get fit. Get fit in the winter for the ski season or in spring so you can boost your immune system. The changing seasons offer us different reasons to embrace life, start fresh, and feel happy."

Gloria, 35, freelance consultant, Sarasota, Florida

If it's because you live somewhere that doesn't have them, travel more. Don't leave a hot and steamy place to go to another. Think outside the box. Head to a ski resort or a lakeside hotel, where you are surrounded by flora and fauna foreign to your usual locale. And remember that there is beauty in the most seemingly mundane of places.

41 Dance Barefoot on the Beach

Women tend to be obsessed with shoes. We talk about them, covet them, enjoy them, and love them, mostly because we stay the same size regardless of how much we've been eating that month.

But sometimes shoes are superfluous in life—and a beach is definitely a place where shoes don't belong. And if you're gonna take your shoes off, you might as well dance. How happy does Ellen DeGeneres look all the time? I'm convinced that has something to do with her continual dancing. Now, if she were dancing on a beach, she'd be as high as a kite.

There's something about the soothing feel of sand between your toes that not only exfoliates away your dead skin but your lingering worries, too. Walking on sand burns 30 percent more calories than walking on a sidewalk; imagine what dancing on sand can do for your bottom.

I once spent a week at a beach resort that had a shoe ban. Being footloose and fancy-free really puts a spring into your step. For some reason, you feel lighter and more able to run and jump and skip and dance. And none of us does enough of that crazy stuff these days.

If you've had a particularly bad month or, God forbid, year, you need to get your sorry ass to a place where you can check your footwear in at the door, grab a rum punch and a hammock, and then dance the night away surrounded by palm trees and other shoe-free, stress-avoidant party people.

Start with the shoes, then build your way up to the point where you don't even care for makeup, jewelry, underwear (live day to night in your bikini), or your cell phone.

Your psyche will thank you for it.

DON'T JUST TAKE IT FROM ME . . .

"Dance like no one is watching. It's one of the most freeing, relaxing, peaceful things in the world. If you're not near a beach, improvise. In your bedroom in front of the mirror with your stereo cranked up to your favorite music you can get some of the same adrenaline going, although a beach is always preferable!"

Jennifer, 31, editor, New York City

"I always have a great time dancing on the beach in Santa Cruz with friends from back home. People have various bongo drums and everyone's high on life, enjoying the sounds of the ocean along with the beats. Dreadlocked hippies dance and drink all night long. Everyone who lives in this area loves these evenings—it's part of the California culture."

Melinda, 29, surf instructor, Los Angeles

IF YOU CAN'T DANCE BAREFOOT ON THE BEACH . . .

Find something else that feels equally freeing to you, something that represents leaving worries at the door. To some women it's forgetting their restrictive diet for a week; for others it's having an alcoholic drink before their usual time of seven o'clock in the evening. For some it will simply be forgetting their hair flatirons and wearing their hair in a ponytail every day. Anything that can make you step away from the mundane and away from the expected is good for the spirit.

42 Take a Deep Breath at Yosemite National Park

We occasionally need to take a chill pill. Where better to swallow that life lesson than in a national park where cell-phone reception is sketchy?

Sometimes it's good to see the world as it is and our role in it realistically. The gigantic expanse of trees, ravines, sunsets, and green life of this great park puts everything in its place. We are vital and so is the environment.

It's hard to focus on the true meaning of global warming and our planet's need for love and attention when your life consists of gray buildings, hard pavements, and workaholics. Take yourself out of your concrete jungle and into an area of great natural beauty, and life becomes clearer. The world is beautiful.

I went to a party a few years ago, and one of the gimmicks to keep you there longer, keep you spending your hard-earned money at the bar, was a wandering aura reader. She saw me and almost cried (I get this a lot—I seem to attract every tarot-card-reading, aura-reading loon in the Western world without encouragement). "You're so green, so green, but it's fading . . . Get yourself to a forest now! Go and hug a tree, for God's sake! Kick your shoes off and feel the grass between your toes before you go mad!"

Even as a child, I was an old soul who took everything and everyone seriously, seeing the world in black and white. My nature is one of earnest contemplation rather than crazy abandon. As I've gotten older, I've noticed that cities encourage this mind-set—yet being in nature diminishes it.

Adding a bit of green does me so much good, and it's a universal unwinding tool that we could all use more often. I took the crazy aura lady's words to heart, and the more I saw green, the less I saw red. And Yosemite is truly one of the great destinations in the United States.

DON'T JUST TAKE IT FROM ME . . .

"The glorious vistas offered in Yosemite are a great place to start. Hiking sounds like hard work, but with the changing landscape

WILDERNESS WOMAN

and a few deep breaths, you'll feel like a new person with a new world unfolding in your lap."

Elizabeth, 24, copywriter, San Francisco

"Sometimes it's nice not to talk, or hear cars, or hit the sidewalk running. That's when I head to a national park or forest like Yosemite. And that's how I stay sane."

Liza, 33, freelance business consultant, Tampa

IF YOU CAN'T TAKE A DEEP BREATH AT YOSEMITE NATIONAL PARK . . .

Find space and quiet wherever you can, and breathe deeply and relax. Even if this is just in your back garden, getting outdoors can remind you how the simple things—sunshine on your face, grass beneath your feet, watching ladybugs crawl up your arms—really are the important things in life.

43 Look for Shooting Stars

Oscar Wilde famously declared, "We're all in the gutter, but some of us are looking at the stars." I like this sentiment. We're all down here on earth, going through our random problems and dilemmas, but above us, every night without fail, are glorious bursts of light and heat and beauty. Pure sparkle.

We're too busy watching what's going on around us at ground level that we miss the beauty overhead. Seeing a shooting star brings a childlike moment of joy to anyone following its glittered path. Spotting three in a row brings a fairy tale–like glee to even the most cynical mind.

I once spent one treacherously long bus journey passing the time by looking for shooting stars. In a bid not to spend too much money, I'd decided to take a cheap coach between Sydney and Melbourne, rather than doing the sensible thing and flying. It was even cheaper to do this journey overnight, so with the rest of the passengers asleep and a cramped nine hours of darkness before me, I plugged in my earphones and looked upward. As the Australian night glided past my window, the stars fell like rain and I was bewitched.

How do you spot them? It can be tricky. You might think that a few drinks will help, but to be honest, a boozy brain will just make you drift off to sleep. You need to concentrate. Lying on your back in the darkness is preferable—with a loved one is superb—and you should just stare straight up and focus. Sometimes you'll be dazzled in minutes; other times it will take a few hours. But it's an amazingly relaxing thing to do, so what's the rush?

So when you're on vacation, or even just at home on a clear, warm night, turn off the television and head outside. Look up, look for the constellations, and wonder at the beauty of it all.

DON'T JUST TAKE IT FROM ME . . .

"One of the most amazing nights of my life to date was going up to Enchantment Resort in Sedona, Arizona, during a meteor shower. I sat outside on the balcony of our bungalow with one of my best guy friends. We sat together in our bathrobes in the most comfortable silence, drinking wine and watching stars fall out of the sky like rain. I made three wishes on stars that night, and I swear within a week of our return to civilization they all came true."

Katie, 29, historian, New York City

"One time in London, I sat in Trafalgar Square on the lions with my ex-boyfriend—it was so romantic. I think I've only ever looked at stars with ex-boyfriends. We were there for about an hour, just staring upward."

Cacey, 36, mechanic, Martha's Vineyard, Massachusetts

IF YOU CAN'T LOOK FOR SHOOTING STARS . . .

Follow the movements of the moon. The eclipses lead us more than we're aware. Our bodies are made up of 90 percent water, and you know what the moon does to the tide, so what does it do to our moods? Google it—there are so many fascinating things to do (or not to do) depending on the phases of the moon.

44 Take a Road Trip

Do you find that you're always in a rush? There are places to go, people to see, things to do. It all gets a bit stressful. Even on vacation, we rush to the airport to make the flight and get through customs and find our luggage at the other end. It's a well-researched statistic that couples argue more at airports than anywhere else, despite the fact that in theory they're doing something wonderful together—taking a vacation.

So what about avoiding the rush-rush, see-see of the usual vacation and taking to the open road? There's something rather old-fashioned and romantic about a meandering trip through a chosen region, booking into little guesthouses on the way. Or suddenly changing your mind about a route or destination and being free to spice things up.

When I was twenty-one years old, I did the usual British twenty-something rite of passage: I went to Australia. After a few weeks, my friend and I were bored of flying from city to city, doing the tourist things, getting drunk in a few bars, and moving on. So we decided to slow things down a bit. We took a ferry to Tasmania, the island off the coast of Melbourne, and rented a beat-up, old bright green Volkswagen Beetle. We found a map somewhere but dismissed it as superfluous whenever we saw a pretty view in the distance. We didn't have a clue where we were most of the time, but getting lost just gave us a chance to talk to the locals. The only downside to the road trip was the number of Tasmanian devils we crushed under the wheels while turning steep bends in the forests (I do regret that). But the actual car cruise was delightful and freeing—and I think every girl needs to feel a little Thelma and Louise (minus the cliff, of course) in her life at least once, don't you?

DON'T JUST TAKE IT FROM ME . . .

"I don't take the path that anyone else has taken. That's my motto for my life—and for my vacations. I have a stressful job, and I need to run everything like clockwork and organize more than twenty people. So in my spare time, I fill my RV with every luxury and treat I can imagine and my husband and I rock and roll our way around the country. The only thing I plan is the music we'll be listening to as we hit each state. I do like driving sound tracks."

Sandra, 40, hotel manager, Little Rock, Arkansas

"My gardening club organized a horticultural trip to Mystic, Connecticut, and we decided to rent a car and drive all the way back to Atlanta when we were done. There were American flags everywhere, and every person we encountered on the way back was warm and welcoming. Driving from state to state in our country was a truly moving experience."

Stella, 53, wholesale-gifts manufacturer,
Atlanta, Georgia

IF YOU CAN'T TAKE A ROAD TRIP . . .

Take a vacation on a train. I acknowledge that driving can be a stressful pursuit, so let someone else take the pressure of getting you slowly from A to B while avoiding airports. Even a four-hour train ride from, say, Washington DC to New York can be fun, if you pack some great food and magazines and let your eyes gaze out the window as the world dashes past. Train stations tend to drop you off in the heart of a city, too, so you don't have that less-than-scenic taxi ride from the airport to the center of town when you arrive.

45 Feed Stingrays

There's a lot lurking under the sea. Luckily, some of these creatures seem to kinda like us. Stingrays have the surprising nickname "teddy bears of the sea." If you squirt a bit of squid juice in a stingray's direction, expect a bit of hugging and holding as it follows its favorite fragrance.

As unlikely as it sounds, it's quite nice getting a little bump and grind from a ray. Stingrays feel like giant, wet mushrooms, the smoothest things you will ever feel in your life (even smoother than a well-moisturized baby's bottom!) and the gentlest, too.

Of course, there is the dreaded tail. But the key is education, and I soon realized that when treated with respect and left in their safe environment, these creatures truly are harmless teddy bears.

If they sting you, they die. They don't want to attack and will do so only if they feel they are being attacked first. What they really want is an easy breakfast in the form of tiny fish or bits of squid.

Feeding them feels a bit ghoulish at first. But most stingrays—even those in the middle of the Pacific Ocean or Caribbean Sea—know what the arrival of a boat means. Rather than being petrified of a gaggle of tourists floating around their neighborhood, they swim up to investigate, expecting a tasty treat. Stingrays look as if they have a permanent grin, which makes them even more lovable—and makes it easier to get over the fact that you are communicating with these wild oceanic beasts, some of which can be up to eight feet long!

Don't feel you have to feed them through their smiles, on their undersides, though. You're more likely to get a harmless nip this way. When I experienced this pleasure, we were taught to drop bits of seafood delight into their gills—those two holes that look like eyes on the top of their head. I'd pop a fish in, get a quick cuddle and swoosh, and turn around to find another one queuing up for a treat. At one point I was surrounded and couldn't do anything but laugh and wonder at how easily we were communicating.

Wear a snorkel to witness the remarkable sight of these flying underwater cruisers as they come to investigate your wares, but never wear flippers. It's too easy to trap or injure one of them with these unruly shoes on!

And go on, give them a cuddle back.

DON'T JUST TAKE IT FROM ME . . .

"They are funny things, stingrays. Being with these beautiful fish reminds you of nature, and real life, and fresh air, and waves and the sky. My whole adult life, I'd only paid attention to fish when I was ordering from a restaurant menu. This reminded me of how the whole world works together—or against one another."

Roberta, 32, writer, Brooklyn, New York

"I found myself in a stingray sandwich once. Two of these smiley creatures realized I was a good source of supper and were fighting over my attention. The smaller of the two got impatient and tried to nibble on my tummy but soon realized I wasn't as tasty as the mahimahi I was dropping into their gills. I still have a tiny scar, which I'm so proud of. Prospective boyfriends are very impressed by my war injury—not realizing it didn't hurt at all—and swimming with these funny fish was the best moment of my life."

Dann, 40, actor, New York City

IF YOU CAN'T FEED STINGRAYS . . .

Get an aquarium at home and fill it with beautiful fish. Studies show that just watching fish swim around is one of the quickest de-stressors you can have. Make sure the tank is big and filled with interesting objects and that you have the proper food and maintenance, then sit back and relax with nature's most chill species.

46 Go on an African Safari

"Hakuna matata," sang that fuzzy little Disney meerkat with his warthog pal. It means no worries (for the rest of your days), but if you seriously want to be without worries for the rest of your days, you should get out into nature.

There is something about the grandness of the African plains that will leave you feeling awestruck, alive, and ultimately very, very small. And that isn't a bad thing. Aren't we all a little guilty of thinking the world revolves around us or that our issues are huge and insurmountable? Standing on a rock, facing the vast expanse of life and light that is the African landscape, will leave you breathless and humble.

Going on a safari makes you feel as though you've been plugged into an electric socket. Suddenly your whole body becomes aware of its more natural needs—you wake with the sun and sleep when the moon appears. You eat simply and drink water. The fresh air and physicality allow you to sleep soundly and stress free. Your mind quiets (without the need for a yoga teacher) as you bathe, looking out onto a canopy of trees and the creatures hidden within its branches.

You return to your own concrete jungle feeling lighter. You've seen this other world that exists only a plane journey away, a land where nature still rules and humans can learn lessons of pride, loyalty, and strength from the greater creatures around them. When you go, as I sincerely hope you do, don't just take photos—too many Safaristas spend their whole time in Africa looking through a camera lens. Capture key moments, sure, but for the rest of the time sit back, observe, be still, and think.

DON'T JUST TAKE IT FROM ME . . .

"The elephants at the Chobe River in Botswana had a bigger impact on me than the Grand Canyon or Niagara Falls. As far as the eye can see, family groups of two or three hundred elephants move slowly along, holding on to one another's tails and helping one another along. The male zebra protects his family group in such an old-fashioned way that it's remarkable. It's worth paying for a professional guide and tracker who can get you close to the animals safely. We drove ten feet from a lion and his lioness. The guide told us as long as we stayed in the Jeep, the lion would think of us as a big animal he couldn't take on. He wouldn't see us as something he could eat!"

Helen, 50, homemaker, London

"You must see the sunsets. African sunsets produce colors I have never seen in the sky before. Every night, wherever we were across Africa, we'd stop at sunset for a gin and tonic. With the chinking of ice in our ears and the soft lime fragrance filling our nostrils, we'd watch the sun drop into the sea or into the land and feel our worries melt away with the heat of the day. It was the best vacation I've ever had. You can't die without seeing Africa. Please!"

Karen, 45, personal assistant,
Sacramento, California

IF YOU CAN'T GO ON AN AFRICAN SAFARI . . .

Check out the National Geographic and Discovery channels on the television or rent the Planet Earth series on DVD. You can get sucked into an afternoon of reality TV, but surely there is no greater reality than life on earth. And you can learn interesting facts to amuse dinner-party guests or to teach your children one day. If one particular animal takes your fancy, contribute to a charity that is seeking to secure that animal's future in the world. They will send you updates, which will make Africa come to you.

47 Swim with Sharks

You think I'm nuts for suggesting this, right? You've spent a few nights as a child cowering behind the sofa as the *dun-dun, dun-dun, dun-dun* music of *Jaws* warned you that something nasty was going to happen. And you think anything that swims in the sea and has big fangs should be avoided at all costs.

Right? Wrong!

If you research reputable tour companies and pay attention when you go on your expedition, it's a safe and worthwhile challenge. Everyone I know who has swum with sharks has it down as her or his number-one thrill of all time. I'm going to sound even crazier when I suggest that sharks have been misrepresented through the camera lenses and puppetry of Hollywood, but it's true. Humans have indeed been killed in shark attacks, but you're more likely to die fishing than by being attacked by a giant fish. There is something so symbolically brave about swimming with sharks that you'll feel stronger and more vibrant the minute you take a plunge into the big, deep blue.

Outside of an aquarium, I first encountered these sleek sea creatures in the Maldives. I'd delight every morning in strolling down the wooden deck of my hotel, iPod in my ears spinning out some soulful tunes, to gaze into the ocean beneath me. I'd stop and spy on the colorful flurries of tropical fish darting between the rocks and seaweed and dangle my feet over the edge to graze the water and keep cool.

One morning as I was doing this, I heard a loud splash—and I know it must have been loud because I heard it clearly over the new Morrissey album I'd downloaded for my trip. I ripped the earphones out and searched beyond my toes for the cause of such a disturbance. Through the turquoise translucence I saw an aquatic scuffle, an oceanic equivalent of a bar brawl. A reef shark was squabbling with a barracuda over a piece of snapper! The barracuda had the snapper clasped tightly in its scissor jaw, and its blood had formed a red cloud around it, attracting the shark. They fought and struggled and snapped at each other until the barracuda gave in to the more powerful king of the water and left hungry.

Now, rather than being put off by the bloodied water and killing creature at my feet, I jumped in to get a closer look. The shark was beautiful, truly like a silver sports car—fast, clean, and made for speed. He devoured the fish and swam between my legs (I kid you not!) and out past the reef. That was a real "wahoo" moment.

That first encounter has led me to many more moments of shark excitement: watching them follow my cruise ship around the Caribbean, throwing them fish at night from a pier in Mauritius, diving with them in Egypt . . . and still the only one that has ever made me jump is Steven Spielberg's mechanical one at Universal Studios.

DON'T JUST TAKE IT FROM ME . . .

"Our Tahitian tour guide told us to get our snorkels in position and jump into the ocean. My knees started to wobble and I had a flicker of doubt. Why did I sign up to swim with sharks? Before I could have a full-on panic attack, I was off the boat and in the freezing water. Looking down into the fifty-foot abyss, I saw circling shadows and then a theatrical swoop about twenty feet in front of me as my first shark won the chunk of tuna thrown from our boat into the sea. As they gathered for these easy pickings, the sharks ignored us bloodless and still humans, allowing us to see them up close in their natural habitat."

Layla, 31, travel editor, Maui, Hawaii

"For some reason, I'd always wanted to get into a cage and be dropped into an ocean filled with sharks. I kept being scared off until I saw photos of elderly Elizabeth Taylor taking the challenge. So I went for it. It was the scariest experience of my life— my heart was beating so loudly in my chest, I thought it was going to escape through my wet suit. It was the biggest adrenaline rush I had ever had. Why go to the effort of bungee jumping when nature offers you this?"

Andy, 28, accountant, Houston, Texas

IF YOU CAN'T SWIM WITH SHARKS . . .

Go swimming with dolphins instead! You can even do this in America, so you won't have to go too far. It does feel a little more sanitized and touristy, but it is still an amazing experience. I've been thrown through the air after balancing on the nose of a dolphin. I lost my bikini bottoms when I hit the water, but the shame was worth it. I've just had to burn the video evidence.

48 Go Skiing in the Winter

Skiing is truly one of the most exhilarating, breathtaking (and rosy glow–inducing) things you can do. Thank you, Mother Nature and the man who invented sticks to glide on.

Now, I am not a natural skier and I am not a classic snow bunny. One of my brothers lovingly refers to me as having "all the gear but no idea" to his smarty-pants snowboarding mates, whose main occupation on the slopes seems to be terrorizing the wobbly kneed by tearing past with their iPods on.

I am more what you'd call a snail skier. I move so slowly, it's surprising I stay upright. But that suits me. And you know why? It's because I was thirty the first time I put a pair of skis onto my feet. I thought I wouldn't be able to do it and always avoided trips to the slopes, preferring instead to escape my seasonal affective disorder with jaunts to warmer climates.

But due to the demands of the aforementioned snowboarding brother, I ventured out onto the mountains and never looked back. I admit I did look down with fear a little for the first few days.

If you are inspired to take up this winter sport, hire a seriously sexy instructor to take your mind off those first few days, which will typically include the following: numbness, sore limbs, a bruised bottom, painful cramps, panic attacks, crying fits, moments of pure horror, and an irrational fear of failure (especially when trying to disembark a moving ski lift without falling over, thereby being hit on the head by the next one). Because when you're past all that—as I now am—a world of marshmallow grilling and hot-tub heaven awaits. It's called *après-ski,* and it's surely the greatest thing the French ever invented.

Après-ski is a lovely thing for any young woman to indulge in and should be tried out even if you do not deem yourself sufficiently sporty to take the skiing bit of the day too seriously. Do what I do: justify your night of sipping pinot noir in front of a log fire by making two trips down an easy green run in the morning. If you fall over, reward yourself with a trip to a spa for a body massage, complete with aromatherapy oils, so that your night of après-ski is not threatened.

I very nearly missed out on skiing. I thought I couldn't do it. Thank heavens I rectified that mistake, because there's no business like snow business.

DON'T JUST TAKE IT FROM ME . . .

"In the office I'm a dork. I don't mind admitting it. I come in, do my work, behave, and go home. Weekends are spent being the good girl: I go to the gym, avoid Oreos, clean my apartment. But then December rolls around and I check snow reports up north, and when I get a few inches, I'm gone. I hit the slopes and become a speed demon. I get color in my cheeks, the wind in my hair, and a buzz that lasts till March."

Katie, 29, mortgage adviser, Cleveland

"Don't just think of skiing as a workout or the chance to buy cute warm gear in pastel shades. I'm naughty to admit it, but it's a great way to meet men—and not just any old men, but exciting, sporty, and daring ones! They're the usual types I meet on the ski lift. Everyone's a winner."

Stephanie, 36, lawyer, Colorado Springs, Colorado

IF YOU CAN'T SKI IN THE WINTER . . .

At least get some après-ski going, even if it's nowhere near a mountain. Decorate your place with twinkly lights, turn the heat up, gather a few friends round for warm cider (or Baileys Irish cream or a hearty bottle of red), and discuss the Flying Tomato. Snow on, you know you want to . . .

JET-SETTER

49 Take an Unforgettable Train Journey

The idea of a trip on a train evokes a Victorian charm and old-school elegance not afforded by other modes of transport. Chugging along, its steam forming clouds, and a toot-toot to greet passersby, the train is a romantic way to reach any destination without that dirty, grubby feeling planes give you—or without the headache (or need for a toilet) of being stuck in a car.

A few years ago, I took an overnight train from London to Edinburgh, the capital of Scotland—a city featuring a grand castle and winding cobbled alleyways. It was fitting that as we wove our way through the gardens of England up north, I lay huddled in my little carriage, wrapped up in thermal pajamas and reading the latest Harry Potter. It had been released that week, and I'd excitedly purchased it for the journey. Awakened at dawn with a knock at the door and a cup of tea, I felt surprisingly refreshed. Train beds are tiny bunkers and the sheets are scratchy, but the constant motion offers a good night's rest. I sat up as we pulled into the station, admiring all my fellow passengers as they trotted off with their luggage, obeying the conductor's whistle to move quickly towards the exit. The seven hours had passed so simply that I was ready to take on a weekend in Edinburgh with gusto—haggis, hairy men in kilts, deep-fried Mars bars . . . and a few more fights with wizards during my downtime. What's not to love?

DON'T JUST TAKE IT FROM ME . . .

"People always think that flying is the easiest way to travel. It may be the quickest, but it's certainly not the easiest. Just getting through security can get me down. Now when I travel between my new life in New York and my old family base in Boston, I take the Acela Express rather than heading to JFK. I choo-choo past Providence and past the lobster huts, and my ears don't get blocked!"

Amber, 25, banking assistant, New York City

"I was eight years old, and my mother and I were going home from Washington State to Indiana. She asked if I wanted to fly or take the train. I said train because I wanted to see America. It was amazing; steaming through the Rocky Mountains was so memorable. The train goes through them and around them, and the mountains are covered in cloud. It took about four days, and I learned how to play gin rummy to pass the time with fellow passengers. I still remember talking to so many amazing people."

Nicole, 33, musician, Sacramento, California

IF YOU CAN'T TAKE AN UNFORGETTABLE TRAIN JOURNEY . . .

At least make your plane or car trip as comfortable as possible. Leave enough time to get to the airport without stressing, pack snacks (you know the food is going to be disgusting and expensive), and wear comfy, loose clothing, bringing a cozy wrap to snuggle with.

50 Shop Till You Drop in New York City

The natural stylishness of Jackie Onassis and Coco Chanel has certainly passed me by. Hell, I'm not even as naturally stylish as an Olsen twin heading to Starbucks after a night at Teddy's in Hollywood. I can't see how colors and fabrics work together to make me look slim, groomed, and attractive.

So when I arrived in NYC armed with a bit of cash and an empty closet, I knew I needed to find a personal shopper. My new job required my (properly attired) presence in meetings, at parties, and on television. Without some help, I'd appear less like an editor in chief and more like a scruff in heap.

Walking into Henri Bendel was intimidating. The trinkets and boxes twinkled from every surface. The poised shop assistants looked so elegant that they could have just as easily been used as mannequins and placed in the windows overlooking Fifth Avenue and no one would have noticed. I clumsily pulled myself up the twisting, ornate staircase to the women's fashion area—in search of the man who was going to save me and my style.

There he was, a flamboyant queen, *au naturelle- ment,* dressed in pleather and giving me the evil eye, clearly unimpressed with the outfit I was wearing. My personal shopper. He twirled me round the store as if we were entering a mini marathon, then dumped me into a changing room with a glass of water. While I recovered and thought, *What the hell have I done,* my PS gathered up the latest designs and brought them back to me.

This was when I began my affair with shopping. No queuing, no searching for sizes, no waiting for a space to try something on. He did all the rushing and carrying and checking while I sat (I'm sure they'd have brought me a cappuccino and a few cookies if I'd asked), saying yea or nay and occasionally falling in love with something and trying it on. The personal-shopper changing room was nicely lit and roomy, and a gaggle of assistants was on hand to praise an outfit—or quietly dissuade me from an item that made my bottom look the size of Texas.

The pièce de résistance was the seamstress who appeared every time I was about to put away my credit card because something was too short, too long, or too tight. Dropping to her knees, she would adjust the hem or let out the lining so seamlessly (excuse the pun) that the item felt as if it had been made for me.

I dropped a lot of cash that day, but I felt like a queen and have been back every time I've needed to look and feel fabulous.

That's the thing about New York City. Not only do the shops there import the best items from around the world, the sales assistants are the best in the world, too. Shopping is a religion. You won't find more alluring products anywhere in the world . . . or more dangerously seductive sellers!

DON'T JUST TAKE IT FROM ME . . .

"People think about shopping in New York as being all about designer goods and expensive Fifth Avenue department stores. It's so not. Head out to Brooklyn. The small boutiques and vintage stores of Williamsburg and Brooklyn Heights are fabulous and reasonable, and they have great bakeries to recharge you when you need a sugar rush."

Clare, 36, stylist, Brooklyn, New York

"I go twice a year from London because I've worked out that what I save in the great discount stores and Chinatown thrift shops more than covers the cost of my flight—and I get to see my lovely American friends, too."

Rose, 33, risk analyst, London

IF YOU CAN'T SHOP TILL YOU DROP IN NEW YORK CITY . . .

Hit up the Web sites of the major Big Apple stores. Bloomingdale's and Barneys are legendary, of course, and many other great brands started in the city. Even if you're stuck miles away from anything but a farm and gas station, stay on trend by treating yourself to virtual window shopping on the Web—with the occasional must-have purchase.

51 Show a Visitor Around Your Hometown

Traveling is life's greatest pleasure, I believe, but sometimes we're so busy planning our next trip that we forget to stop and appreciate where we are. Living in a foreign country has truly allowed me to fall in love with my homeland in a way many people can never do.

Hey, I admit, being a born and bred Londoner is a blessing—and I always knew that. Not only is England a historical, architectural, and creative hot spot for all things bloody lovely, it's also really just a hop, skip, and a jump across the sea to France, Scotland, Ireland, and so on. A weekend in Copenhagen? Easy. Lunch in Brussels? Sure. Fancy the opera in Verona next Wednesday? Done.

I always felt lucky, but my true hometown pride came when I started bringing Americans back to Blighty with me to stay with my parents.

My assistant, Derek, is an adorable young Anglophile who, until he started working for me, had never left the country. I encourage all my team to travel, and we have a vacation feature in every issue of *OK!* magazine that is written by a member of the staff. After a year in the office, Derek had been to Belize and the Caribbean, but as a major Spice Girls and Harry Potter fan, he'd always really wanted to go to England. Working with a bunch of Brits at *OK!* had whetted his appetite further, despite our stiff upper lips and Cadbury brain freezes.

Planning Derek's trip to London with me was as much fun as planning an exotic vacation somewhere I'd never been before. We'd devour maps of landmarks and tourist walks, and I'd fill him in on what princess lived here and what writer lived there. By the time we finally got to the capital, I was as excited as a child on Christmas morning. Yes, apart from my recent three years in New York and three years of studying in the ancient cathedral city of Canterbury, I'd always lived in London and knew its cobbled streets and dingy pubs like the back of my hand. But seeing it through the eyes of a tourist made it all new and exciting again.

Ask the person you're welcoming what she or he has heard about your hometown and where she or he would like to explore. A new visitor can help you discover places you didn't even know existed. Seeing home through a new pair of eyes can help you realize what makes you proud, what makes you a little embarrassed, and what makes you happy to call it home. Guiding a stranger can often guide you back to the truth: that home really is where the heart is.

DON'T JUST TAKE IT FROM ME . . .

"I love when friends from my hometown come and visit me in New York. I came here for college and never left, so even though it's not the place where I was born, it has become part of my soul. I am so proud to know where to get the best curry or pizza, and having visitors reminds me of that."

Katie, 28, writer, New York City

JET-SETTER

"Taking people home not only reintroduces you to local places and bars that you may have forgotten about, it also helps you look at your family and friends with fresh eyes. Sometimes this is bad news and you end up begging to get out of the place, but mostly it makes you appreciate what you've got."

Tania, 32, musician, Topeka, Kansas

IF YOU CAN'T SHOW A VISITOR AROUND YOUR HOMETOWN . . .

Don't wait until you have someone to impress—you could be waiting forever. Find out about local-history classes and events in your area. There's always something going on under your nose. Check out listings in local newspapers. Nature trails on the outskirts of town offer beautiful sights and a fun way to get fit.

52 People Watch in Paris

Watching old men smoke cigarettes in an ambient café while ladies in tight black chemises sip espressos and lean in to gossip conspiratorially is a delicious way to spend time. While the world rushes past, Paris—as a city—sits and contemplates the drama, the upset, the glamour, and the vibrancy.

Sitting alone at a table can be uncomfortable in other cities. In the French capital, however, it's not only acceptable and unexceptional, it's as delightful as watching an artist throw down his paints onto a canvas to see what emerges. Paris in springtime—or any other time of year, for that matter—is a painting come to life. You feel more creative and as if you can understand the world and its dramas just by breathing in the air.

In my life, few things have been more fun than spying on lovers squabbling in corners at the Musée de l'Orangerie or admiring the confidence of the seductive women choosing lingerie for their new lovers at the Galeries Lafayette. Taking the train from the suburbs of Cormeilles-en-Parisis into the Gare du Nord provided many insights into the day-to-day life of the French and the passion with which they do everything.

It would be too un-British of me to pretend that we've always seen eye to eye with *Les Frogs,* as we like to call them (it's not one-sided—they refer to us as *Le Ros Boeuf,* after our obsession with having a Sunday roast dinner). In fact, my first few trips to Paris were difficult, to say the least. Between the ages of eleven and eighteen, I headed there every April to stay with a French family. Every year I boarded the plane with an overwhelming sense of sophistication. Even as a preteen, I knew how brave and fabulous I was being, heading to Paris to learn a new language when my other friends were scared to go to the shops on their own. I relished the education it afforded me, the strengthening of the soul, and certainly my French teacher liked that she had someone to talk to in class at last!

Mais zut alors! Ma bonne amie était horrible! My little French pen pal was a total meanie and clearly didn't want her summers hampered by this geeky little English kid who arrived on her doorstep each April. She wanted to be smoking her Gitanes and listening to Vanessa Paradis with the boy from next door. Instead, my arrival meant educational visits to the Louvre and Versailles. Even worse, when she went to school, I had to go with her. Poor kid. It must have been embarrassing for her. Despite being a nerd and studying hard, I still spoke her language with a thick Cockney accent, and her friends would giggle.

This is when I became obsessed with just watching. I'd do her a favor and disappear for the afternoon to allow her to regain some cool. Slipping out onto the streets with no particular place to go, I'd sit in parks and cafés and watch the world go by. I'd count hundreds of tiny little dogs, thousands of bristly women carrying baguettes, millions of children being rushed between classes in neat navy bibs. The city is a Cézanne in reality—a landscape of beauty to be looked at, rather than understood.

I didn't feel a part of the city until the minute I stopped trying to figure it all out. Then, as soon as I stopped, I got it. And it really got me.

DON'T JUST TAKE IT FROM ME . . .

"For a fashionista, Paris is heaven. It's the center: it has the best fashion week, and all the couture houses are there. Style is ingrained in the streets and on the sidewalks. I would love to go back."

Marielle, 30, fashion buyer, New York City

"As a city, Paris always fulfills my expectations. It never changes. You could jump into a time machine, go back to 1955, and everything would look the same. It is not a city beholden to fleeting trends or fashions like New York or London."

Briony, 31, designer, Dublin

You can indulge your nosy side outside of Gay Paree. I love sitting with a coffee (or an ice-cream cone on a hot day), regarding the ebbs and flows of life going on around me. It's like reality television in front of your face, without a hideous sound track or snooty host. I often have to watch that I don't chuckle to myself and look like a mad woman.

53 Say Yes to a Night Out with Locals

Jet lag and general travel fatigue are annoying things. You plan a trip for months, sometimes years, and then the minute you hit the fresh soil—bed is all you want to see, and sleep is all you want to do. How terribly, terribly dull.

It's easy to give in to this urge to rest. I've suffered with jet lag and tiredness that made me feel as though I were swimming through a sea of maple syrup. But the more I've traveled, the more I've realized sleep is for wimps. I take inspiration from the lovely Lionel Richie, who recommended not only dancing on the ceiling, but partying all night long.

When you land on foreign turf and you meet locals who invite you out with them, say yes—regardless of how you feel. You can always sleep tomorrow. However good your guidebook and tour operator are, they are not going to know the true hidden secrets of a city.

Getting to know the people who live there is the best way to escape tourist traps and stereotypes and live on the wild side.

I'm not suggesting you go home with your new mate (the friendly chap who turns out to be the local drug lord), but I am encouraging safe entertainment in a group, with people who really know the area.

A few years ago, I visited Iceland with some English friends. We'd read a few leaflets and spoken to a few fellow Brits who'd visited the year before, so we knew we had to go and swim in the Blue Lagoon and have cocktails at Björk's bar. Luckily for me, one of my travel buddies (an actor who was taking a few months off to "grow a beard for a part") happened to be dating Miss Iceland.

This transformed our trip. Suddenly, the beauty queen and her Nordic chums were taking us for an evening of Icelandic decadence not mentioned in the guidebooks. Hipster bars, crazy streets, a gourmet gastrodome with the local mayor—and a party back at her flat, where we downed 80-proof shots and ate rotting shark.

Okay, so the last bit wasn't too wonderful. And getting up for a sunrise pony ride through the glaciers certainly wasn't pretty (well, I wasn't—I think I got only two hours' sleep!). But it was worth it. I look shocked in all the vacation photos and I think I came down with the flu when I got home, but I saw true Iceland. And it was every bit as cool as its name would suggest.

DON'T JUST TAKE IT FROM ME . . .

"My friends and I spent a fabulous twenty-four hours in Greece a few years ago, avoiding the tourist bars and taking time to smash plates, an ancient Greek tradition. We randomly befriended some fishermen and went to their family-run restaurant for great food and music. The fact they had a few sexy sons also helped!"

Hayley, 33, homemaker, London

"Philadelphia can seem like a rather flat historical place if you don't know where to go. But with locals, it's ringing a lot more than the Liberty Bell. Despite being exhausted and enticed by the room-service menu, I joined locals and we went round to the Irish pubs, then hit up a legendary Philly cheesesteak place at three in the morning. I didn't like the Cheez Whiz too much, but everything else was cool."

Emily, 30, public-relations executive, Trenton, New Jersey

IF YOU CAN'T SAY YES TO A NIGHT OUT WITH LOCALS . . .

Question the concierge. Don't rely on tourist traps and formulaic travel guides. Ask what's new and where the locals go. And if you're tired, just drink some espresso, already. You only live once.

54 Hit Bourbon Street (but Don't Wait for Mardi Gras)

Venturing into the heart of New Orleans's French Quarter is like leaving America and stepping into a different world. Sure, you can find a McDonald's or Starbucks if you search for one, but by and large it's not just the architecture here that is European. It's the attitude, too. And in a land of monotonous drive-throughs and shopping malls, this is a rather good thing.

Tourists and party people tend to think that the only time worth going to New Orleans is during Mardi Gras, that crazy week in late winter or early spring when girls are encouraged to flash their chests in return for some brightly colored beads. Being a bit of a prude, I think this seems like the perfect reason to skip this time and instead go there when it's not so chaotically naked. There's *always* a naughty feel in the air. You might not be requested to strip any other time of year, but no fear—you'll still have fun.

The famous strip of bars in N'awlins is aptly named Bourbon Street. On ground level, you'll encounter a Day-Glo bar, followed by a seedy strip club, interrupted by a po'boy take-out joint followed by yet another Day-Glo bar. This continues on both sides of the street for about half a mile. It's marvelous.

I went there last Thanksgiving with two friends. The minute we checked into the hotel, we felt at home. Considering the monumental problems the city has had since Hurricane Katrina, the atmosphere was nothing but warm and welcoming with a pervading sense of energy.

A sedate glass of champagne in the Ritz Carlton bar was in order to plan our attack of this party capital. With a map sprawled out in front of us, we knew our end point had to be the mecca of all funsters—Pat O'Brien's, the legendary home of the Hurricane, the most lethal cocktail on the planet. "Only have one—it'll send you over the edge," veteran LSU alumni had warned me before the trip. What nonsense! I was British. We knew how to hold our liquor. Or so I thought.

Hitting the strip on a chilly day in November sounds miserable, but the atmosphere was that of a carnival, Christmas Day, and prom night rolled into one. In the first bar, my friends decided to go lightly. I thought, *Sod it, I'm here,* and ordered a bucket of Jack Daniel's and Diet Coke (sure, the fact that it was diet was gonna help!).

"You want that in a take-out bucket, darlin'?" the cowboy boot–sporting lady behind the bar inquired.

Well, hell yeah!

Fifteen photos of me posing with a giant plastic beaker later and we scarpered onward, through the throngs of the boozed-up (we are now among them so we think they all look rather beautiful), singing, laughing, and daring one another to go into a strip bar, until suddenly there it was, like a vision in the desert: Pat O'Brien's, home of the Hurricane.

"Three Hurricanes, please," we announced—as if

any visitor has ever ordered anything else. The barman pumped bright red liquid straight from a massive barrel into three tourist-friendly tankards. The recipe is so secret that even the bar staff doesn't know what we're being served. First sip: nice. Second sip: rather splendid. Third sip: wahoooo—party time!

At this point things got a little too fun and frisky. In order to protect my friends, I will not divulge any more information from this evening. I don't mind embarrassing myself, but I have these two dear people's reputations to consider.

Needless to say, my night out on Bourbon Street was probably the most fun I've had in my three years of living in the United States. I've been lucky enough to meet George Clooney at the Golden Globes, dance with Sharon Stone at the Oscars, and go behind the scenes at New York Fashion Week, but nothing compares to N'awlins.

DON'T JUST TAKE IT FROM ME . . .

"It's like going to Tijuana without having to take your passport—it's like another country. The second a barman says, 'You want your gin and tonic in a to-go cup?' you know you're in a crazy place. Everyone's on vacation, even the locals. Anything goes and all are welcome in New Orleans."

Shona, 25, party planner, Malibu, California

"New Orleans needs tourist dollars. It needs to be restored and celebrated. This must be the only city in the United States where you can drink a cocktail while wandering the streets with a smug grin on your face. What's stopping you from booking your flight?"

Laura, 31, travel writer, Los Angeles

The fainthearted won't relish what the strip has to offer, so if that's you, steer clear. But the city still has a wealth of things to explore. Indulge in coffee and beignets at Café du Monde on the river and forget this other side of the city exists. Take a carriage ride to admire the architecture, and spend your evenings avoiding drunken revelers by heading to the Snug Harbor jazz restaurant for gumbo and shrimp.

55 Sit Still at Machu Picchu

To get to the historic wonder of Machu Picchu, we embark on a bumpy ride through the Andes, along unfinished roads and past flowering crops of potatoes. Donkeys and dogs jog alongside us, causing us to halt abruptly on occasion. Much buttock gripping ensues. Just as I'm feeling a bit off, my chatty driver announces that it's normally at this point that tourists come down with altitude sickness. I start to feel dizzy and my head feels as though it's trapped inside a donkey's bottom. I transfer onto another bus. "Twenty minutes and we'll be there," the new driver informs me with a maniacal grin . . .

And there it is.

Serene and all conquering.

Surrounded by cloud, forest, and blue sky, the flat ledge of stone and green grass are humbled by the sky-searching mountains encompassing it.

I'm breathless.

My long journey, pain, and discomfort disappear in the face of this absolute moment of peace.

Alberto, our guide, talks on and on about the Incas and their beliefs and tells us that Machu Picchu is the perfect place to worship Mother Nature: the sky, the sun, life and death, rain and rainbows, all meet here.

I hear it but I'm not listening.

The only sound I can hear is that of beauty and spirituality.

I finally place the heavy baggage (physical and emotional) I've been dragging around with me on the rocks beneath my feet. And I sit. Still.

DON'T JUST TAKE IT FROM ME . . .

"They say it's one of the energy centers of the earth where people go 'to find themselves.' I think I was initially looking too hard, but staring over the mountains as the breeze blew through my hair, listening to the complete silence, it was as if time stopped for a minute while I wrote about the experience in my journal. Being on top of Machu Picchu in the morning before the mountain's opened to tourists can feel as though you're the only person in the world."

Jennifer, 32, reporter, Los Angeles

"I'd always dreamed of going to the seven wonders of the world, and Machu Picchu seemed to be the most impossible—something about going to Peru, I suppose. But it didn't disappoint. I had to save up and stay in for a few months to afford the trip, and honestly, it was worth it."

Ann, 35, homemaker, Boston, Massachusetts

Embark on another journey that means something to you. Have you always been drawn to a certain place or people? If so, something inside you is telling you to go. Make sure you do. Making the effort to get places is exhausting and expensive, but seeing the world expands your mind. Apart from the love of family and friends, is there anything more purely joyful than understanding our planet?

56 Gawp at the Taj Mahal

It's 5:30 a.m. and the streets of Agra are already buzzing. Taxi drivers honk their horns, lorries roar down the pot-holed roads, bicyclists ring their bells. Even a confused-looking bull wanders the street (at least it's not making any noise). Beggars wait for tourists, ready to pounce. The sun is barely up, it's getting steamy, and the stress levels are already through the roof.

Then, just ahead you spy the entrance gate, beckoning you into a safe place, far away from the mayhem. You hustle through the entrance, turn the corner, and then silence.

The Taj Mahal.

You've seen it on TV, in films, and depicted on the front of curry-house menus, but none of that can possibly prepare you for the sheer majesty of the place. This gleaming, delicate, wonderful structure sits in front of you, patiently, waiting for you to realize you are looking at something quietly spectacular.

Nobody speaks. It is as if the Taj Majal has put a finger to its lips and whispered a polite *shhh.*

That fresh white sunlight you see only at dawn bounces off the dome, creating a vision of blue, silver, and yellow. The building's perfect symmetry is mesmerizing. Strictly speaking it is a mausoleum, built by an agonized and grieving ruler of India in memory of his late wife more than three hundred years ago. It is history's grandest monument of love. It's quite surprising to be told you're allowed to actually go inside such a place; it feels as if you've been given the go-ahead to hop up onto the catwalk at a fashion show and plant a big wet kiss on one of the models. Inside is great, but not as jaw-dropping as the exterior, so get back outside, find a quiet bench, and gawp.

Whatever mental picture you have of the Taj Mahal in your head, the real thing is infinitely more impressive, more beautiful, more serene; that's why it should be on your list of things to see before you get tied to your hometown with a bunch of kids. It's a seriously unforgettable experience.

And thank God that it is, thank God that it lives up to the hype, because it would be a terrible shame to have battled through the beggars, lorries, and livestock to come face to face with something that makes you say, "Yeah, quite nice. Shall we have lunch?"

DON'T JUST TAKE IT FROM ME . . .

"Go . . . because, despite perhaps your familiarity with the monument from exposure to countless media images, nothing can detract from the sheer awe and wonder the Taj inspires when you first set eyes on it. It's more than just an architectural masterpiece and an example of the finest craftsmanship—it's a tribute to a great love story."

Claire, 33, customer-relations director, London

"I have never had the experience where the beauty of something created by man hypnotically and overwhelmingly intensified with each step taken toward the structure. I've also never had a situation where the buildup of expectation in seeing something as unquestionably famous and unique as the Taj was so inadequate to the actual experience itself."

Billy, 41, banker, Boston

IF YOU CAN'T GAWP AT THE TAJ MAHAL . . .

Investigate another beacon of true love nearer to home. It sounds a little macabre, but I love to visit graveyards to look at the poignant messages left on tombstones by grieving spouses. Nothing makes you realize the true enormity of love and how we should value it every day than learning about those whose hearts no longer beat.

57 Take an Alternative Vacation

Going away for a few days doesn't have to involve hot tubs and hotels. Sometimes giving back when getting away can be more of a break than a few days on a beach. It feels good to embrace another culture—and to lend a hand while you are there.

When I explain that I traveled to Brazil for an educational visit organized by a Christian charity to help the media fully comprehend what awful suffering and inequalities are part of everyday life, you might think I'm mad for loving this country so much. My days were spent in schools, orphanages, hospitals, and homes with no electricity or water, and I was meeting people who had lost their jobs, homes, and families to HIV.

The fact that this is now my favorite country in the world goes some way to tell you how remarkable the people of this South American nation are—and how their lust for life in the face of all that is cruel and difficult in the world rubs off on anyone who is lucky enough to go there for a few weeks and see it for her- or himself.

When we think of Brazil, we tend to think of gorgeous supermodels, soccer stars, and sexy dancers. And they're all there. Women of every color and shape and size dazzle in teeny-weeny bikinis, comfortable in their skin, happy to unleash their dimpled bottoms and cellulite-troubled thighs onto the golden sands of Ipanema. Athletic men, young and old, pause their games of soccer to whistle appreciatively as the women cool off in the sea before continuing their beautiful game, scoring goals worthy of David Beckham. And the air truly is filled with samba beats wherever you go. But the country is more than all the stereotypes.

Taking an alternative vacation, where you get to really understand a country and its struggles—and try in some small way to help—will make you fall in love and appreciate the place and its people even more. Witnessing fellow humans displaying true dignity in the most difficult of times is inspiring. Life throws all sorts at us, and it is the generosity of those around us that can get us through dark times. I learned this from the people of Brazil. You can learn it by taking a charity-led or educational trip anywhere in the world that is different from your own home.

DON'T JUST TAKE IT FROM ME . . .

"Going to South America, for me, was a humbling experience. I am glad I took the trip with a charity group and saw more than the tourist hot spots. It is a continent of amazing contrasts. It is all too easy to overlook the problems that take place there when you are on vacation and faced with beautiful people, scenery, and food. However, scratch the surface and there are so many people struggling to survive with no money and plenty of violence. Good souls have made it their mission to educate and inspire and change things, and I was glad to witness their work up close."

Anna, 31, public-relations manager, London

"What struck me about my time in Bali was the amazing resilience of those living in poverty. From the villages come numerous stories of creativity triumphing over all sorts of material obstacles. I still love it because of the uninhibited social outpouring of revelry in the rich, creative culture."

Julia, 32, charity administrator, Sydney, Australia

Look at where you live with new eyes. Is there a cause that you could help out with? Try volunteering within your own community.

58 Stay Up All Night in Las Vegas

What happens in Vegas stays in Vegas. If you can let your hair down, go crazy, and get naughty anywhere in the world, it's here. I love it!

I wouldn't recommend going to Vegas in a fragile state of mind—or health. This city is going to take it out of you. Fresh air, fresh food, and exercise don't really come into play (unless you count energetic dancing on banquettes).

But if you're feeling reckless, wild, excitable, and in the mood for fun, Vegas is the place to go. It was designed for indulging passions.

The only rule to life on the infamous strip is to not outstay your welcome. I was a judge for the Miss America pageant last year and had to spend eight days there. It was too much. By the third day my skin had gone to pot, by the fourth I was constipated, and by the fifth I tried to escape it all by banging my head on a slot machine. A weekend should do the trick.

But go for it all night long.

Any all-nighter in Vegas should start off with a gondola ride at the Venetian. As you are being punted and sung to, plan the night ahead.

There are a plethora of options for dinner. Every top chef in New York and Los Angeles has opened a fabulous outpost there. For the view, the French bistro Alizé atop the Palms is unbeatable and classy—just don't do the onion soup and the steak because you really won't be able to move. For cool Americana, head to David Burke's place in the Palazzo. Save space for his legendary cheesecake, lollipop tree, and bubble-gum ice cream.

Head to the theater if you fancy chilling out and dozing off your dinner. *Phantom of the Opera* is the Broadway classic of Vegas—it's presented in a shorter party-crowd format in a specially designed auditorium, and it'll knock your socks off. If you're in the mood for a laugh, Rita Rudner is politically incorrect and fabulous. If you fancy a singsong, there's always someone worth seeing headlining at the MGM Grand.

After a show, there's only one cocktail bar where *Sex and the City* meets the Rat Pack meets London chic, and that's Tao. Baths decorated with naked women and rose petals bedeck the entrance, and once inside, a giant Buddha surveys the party people below as they toast their own gorgeousness.

When you've had your fill of spiritual drinking, jump into a taxi (all the hotels in Vegas are so huge that they are deceptively far away from one another) and head to the Bellagio, the home of the famous fountains. Duck inside the Bellagio for its hottest nightspot, the Bank. Fight your way to the DJ booth to request some tunes, then dance the night away. Just before the sun rises, I suggest slipping out to the burger bar in the casino of Planet Hollywood. Go for the barbecue and bacon variety—pair it with a Diet Coke, and your hangover will run scared.

As the sun is rising, grab a helicopter ride and fly toward the Grand Canyon. Taking in one of the greatest sights in America—a natural delight that's only thirty minutes from the fake glamour of the strip—will leave you very calm. As soon as you land in the middle of the ravines, your delicate head will enjoy the silence. And you'll be pleased to know drinking champagne at sunrise surrounded by cacti is optional. Orange juice is fine, too.

And there you have it. One of the most memorable nights of your life.

DON'T JUST TAKE IT FROM ME . . .

"There's something so old-school about Vegas that the minute you walk into one of their fake-lit, fake-oxygenated casinos, you want to smoke cigarettes and flirt with toxic men. I've learned my lesson and now go there only with girlfriends when I'm single. It's not the same with your boyfriend or parents. It has to be girlie, and glamorous, and giddy. And you have to buy new underwear to go there!"

Emma, 31, journalist, London

"I went there for my twenty-fifth birthday and ended up drinking with rock stars, dancing with basketball players, avoiding Playboy bunnies, eating with billionaires . . . it was crazy. Vegas is more celebrity-filled than Hollywood these days. Everyone is just there to have fun, get wasted, and be as naughty as you're legally allowed these days. Don't bother with the days here—there's nothing to do. Hide out in your dark hotel room until you're ready to throw on a rocking dress and dance till you collapse. It really is the city of fun."

Jenny, 35, public-relations manager, Philadelphia

IF YOU CAN'T STAY UP ALL NIGHT IN LAS VEGAS . . .

Stay up all night in your town! See what happens when the sun goes down and the nocturnal party animals start playing. Yes, you might usually be a couch potato or bed dweller after hours, but at least give it a chance once—even if it means drinking a few caffeine shots to help keep your eyelids open.

59 Go Ghost Hunting in England

There is something so wonderful about stepping back in history and walking the same steps of ancient rulers, infamous villains, heartbroken maidens, and ruthless kings. In old castles and cathedrals about the British Isles, the air is so thick with history—with dramas from another era—you can hardly breathe.

We all know the tales of King Arthur, Henry the VIII and his hopeless and helpless six wives, Robin Hood and his Merry Men, the evil rulers of Olde London Town, Sweeny Todd, and Jack the Ripper. All their stories come alive when you walk around England's twisting cobbled streets.

We English pride ourselves on our history in a mock-flippant way. "Oops, there's another castle," we exhale, as if we aren't proud of these medieval fortresses.

The one thing that worries us a little bit about our gloried, and gory, past is all the spooky-dookyness of the place. England is a ghostbuster's heaven. Things that go bump in the night, headless horsemen, screaming banshees—you name it, we've got it. Go to any pub and strike up a conversation with a local, and he'll fill you in on all the creepy goings-on. Most towns now actually have ghost tours and graveyard walks (a few nips of gin will give you the confidence to sign up).

Ghostly encounters are never far away in England, and that's part of its charm. Every hotel seems to have a tragic love story built into its walls, and there's always a crying sailor to be seen at the witching hour—especially when you've had a few more nips of gin!

I can still feel the hairs on the back of my neck stand up when I remember the time I was lying in bed in a friend's old, old house and felt someone lean over me, breathing heavily. My heart was beating so loudly, I feared it might jump out of my chest. The next day at breakfast, the family shared the secret of the sad gardener, who loved the mistress of this house so much that he didn't believe she'd died. He'd check the house every night for her—especially when a new lady arrived. Yikes!

Nowhere else in the world is history so living and breathing. The stories of these spirits may leave you teary and frightened, but they'll also leave you knowledgeable—and able to cope with a giant marshmallow man in New York City any night of the week!

DON'T JUST TAKE IT FROM ME . . .

"If you like Harry Potter or old British movies—or even *Love Actually* and *The Holiday* movies—you will love going to England and seeing the beauty and the history for yourself. We think we have history here in the United States? No way. My friend took me to her dad's golf club for lunch when I was visiting her—it was more than two hundred years old. The American Constitution could have been signed there—and it was just a golf club!"

Janice, 29, shop assistant, Tulsa, Oklahoma

"I love showing visitors around my country. I feel so proud to have this immense history—lots of it gory and grave, I admit—that is ingrained into every church, manor, and forest. England, for the most part, does have a fairy tale–like charm to it. Go talk to the ladies in tea shops or the men in pubs—hear their village tales of ghost hunting and kings and queens. History really does hang in the air here."

Linda, 43, hospital worker, Liverpool, England

IF YOU CAN'T GO GHOST HUNTING IN ENGLAND . . .

Walk the Freedom Trail in Boston and reward yourself after the three-mile jaunt with a trip to Quincy Market for a cup of lobster bisque and a Boston cream pie. And visit the ghosts of the Founding Fathers— good spirits, all of them!

60 Eat Too Much in Italy

There is a saying, "You eat to live, or you live to eat." I certainly fall into the second category. I honestly think if given the choice between going without sex for the rest of my life or going without another slice of pizza, I'd give up sex. Yes, yes, getting freaky with it is a good way to lighten the mood and keep your partner happy, but does it really fulfill you in the same way as a slice—or three—of deep-dish pepperoni? I think not. So if you're like me, you really must get your arse off to Italy. This is the land that God himself meant you to overindulge in.

Let me put it simply, in a few words: bruschetta, minestrone, parmigiana, linguine, risotto, calamari, mozzarella, spaghetti Bolognese, and pesto. And let me hit you with one more: tiramisu. *Bellissimo!*

And I'm not even going to go on about the wine lists that accompany these delights, but they're long and better than anything we can do in America for the same price.

A very sexy man I know has told me the most important factor he looks at when on a first date is how the woman behaves in a restaurant. If she decadently licks her spoon, guzzles her wine, sucks down oysters, and finishes her steak, he's in love. Maybe that's why the air in Italy is so dripping with romance, flirtation, passion—and the smell of fettuccine Alfredo.

I can recount splendid meals from all of the Italian cities I've visited with the detail of a top chef.

I recall the most succulent lasagna, lukewarm and flavorful, that I devoured in under a minute, sitting at a little wrought-iron table with friends in Verona. A little bit of Veronese heaven.

The gelato is so good in Venice, that when I was a teen I got overexcited making my parents taste it and dropped a scoop down my best dress. When I went back for more, I lost my camera down one of the winding streets, but I didn't care. The cooling mint chocolate chip on my tongue eased my trauma, and I was soon hopping over bridges until I was back in St. Mark's Square, chasing pigeons.

Hot and historic, Rome demands a lot from its tourists. Thankfully, the afternoons can give way to long, leisurely lunches, where sunburned visitors search for shade under the fig trees and marvel at the gorgeous dark men on their Vespas. One afternoon, after tossing too much loose change into the Trevi Fountain, desperate for direction, I headed down a side street for some peaceful contemplation. I found it in a family-run trattoria—a plate of ham, honeydew, and ciabatta and what must have been nearly a liter of a sickly sweet liquor I soon developed a thing for called limoncello.

I cannot push you enough, dear people, to get on a plane to Italy. To soak in the culture—and the Chianti. To feast your eyes on the people—and the ricotta cheesecake. Life is too short to calorie count all the time.

DON'T JUST TAKE IT FROM ME . . .

"Italians do it better. Without a doubt. My first boyfriend was a Long Island Italian dude who spent his vacations in the sun with his family in Sicily. Mealtimes at his place—in the United States and Italy—were loud, bustling times of overindulgence and happiness. Some of the women were voluptuous, but they were sexy and could never resist an extra serving of macaroni. The men were real men, macho and hungry and all too willing to keep the wine flowing. I may not be an Italian, but I try to live like one as much as possible."

Josephine, 35, receptionist, Nashville

"You can't diet in Italy. But why would you? Men appreciate curves and a girl with a sense of adventure. Women admire joie de vivre and a big heart. It's the place to go to kick back and enjoy life. You feel the stress and tensions of everyday small stuff slipping away the minute you step off the plane and get hit by the lemon-scented heady air."

Flavia, 34, copy chief, New York City

IF YOU CAN'T EAT TOO MUCH IN ITALY . . .

Get a good cookbook. *Patsy's Cookbook,* a collection of classic Italian recipes, is a must-have for Mediterranean evenings at home. Sit alfresco if you can, surrounded by tea lights and trees. Ask a swarthy date (or your best friends) to bring some chilled Asti Spumante and to come ready for some fun conversation. Cook up a storm of pasta, pizza, and risottos and buy some cannoli for dessert. Finish with dark and strong Italian coffee and biscotti—and perhaps a good-night kiss!

FREE SPIRIT

61 Get a Vibrator

Plastic fantastic. This is probably the most personal thing included in this book, and it's only thanks to my rather open friends (you know who you are!) that I realized just how empowering sex toys could be.

Vibrators are very decadent. You decide when you need something, how much, and how often, and then you get on with your life. There's no regret, doubt, sleeplessness, wet patch, snoring, and so on.

A real live guy is still better, of course, but when you're man-less, or he's exhausted, or you just need a little bit more, this is a great addition to anyone's life. There's still a taboo surrounding this topic, so make life easy for yourself and order online. You don't have to tell anyone. Hide it in a secret place and coyly deny any knowledge of sex toys whenever the subject comes up. But more people than you imagine have them (even my friends' mums have talked about partaking!), and men are really okay with them. In fact, most men find the idea of a woman taking control of her own pleasure exciting.

DON'T JUST TAKE IT FROM ME . . .

"A few years ago I was having therapy to deal with an eating disorder. In one session my therapist suggested I try the 'distraction' technique—whenever the urge came on to 'partake' in the disorder, I should distract myself. She gave me a list of ideas—from painting to sculpting—but I decided to go for a vibrator instead."

Chrissie, 29, branding manager, London

"It was a strange sense of liberation the day I bought my first vibrator. I proceeded to sit on a packed subway on the way home munching away on my complimentary mint nipples. Had I had some batteries on me, who knows what would have happened!"

Christine, 33, marketing executive, New York City

IF YOU CAN'T GET A VIBRATOR . . .

Check out a naughty Web site or buy yourself some erotic literature. Anaïs Nin always does the job without making you feel sleazy or perverted. If anyone asks, it's erotica, not porn, remember?

62 Spend the Whole Weekend in Bed

Regularly. You know that feeling, when you're in the office or traveling or up early, and you think back to the weekend just passed and wonder why you rushed around so much? Remember that feeling the next time you have a weekend with not much on your schedule, and get back under the covers.

I'm not suggesting a full-on John Lennon and Yoko

Ono–style bed-in. I am just encouraging you to take it slow every now and again. We all hurry. We all feel guilty if we don't get to the gym. We all feel lazy if we let the laundry sit dirty a few days longer than it should. But please. Life should be about the pursuit of pleasure—not just about being in pursuit. Chill out.

To make the most of your weekend in bed, do a bit of planning on the Friday before. Clear your calendar. Finish any nagging work issues that could distract you from your slothlike forty-eight hours. Then, if there's still any time left, get to the gym and do a good, hard workout. This way your sneakers can sit unused all weekend without any flash of guilt on your part.

So what makes the perfect weekend in bed? A few things are key. Your kitchen needs to be stocked with all your favorite foods. And if you intend to survive on ice cream and takeout from your local restaurants, good for you. Have the menus on hand and a freezer full of the good stuff. This is not the weekend for calorie counting—although if you want to use this energy-saving couple of days as a chance to do a raw diet or juice detox, go for it. At least stuck indoors, you'll be out of the way of temptation.

What other items will improve your weekend? Clean sheets and comfy pajamas are a must. You don't have to stay in bed for all forty-eight hours, but you should be in that slow mode—therefore, pajamas and slippers are your uniform. Even if you have to run to your postbox or local store, keep the jammies on— just cover up with a big coat or tracksuit top. Other necessities are a good bubble bath and candles. The only time you're allowed to remove your sleepwear is when you're taking a long, lazy dip in your tub. Warm your muscles and soothe your brain with lavender and eucalyptus oils, and then it's back into the pajamas you go, feeling blissed out and ready for a movie or comedy marathon. Did you miss all the Oscar-nominated films this year? Rent them and educate yourself. Or go lighter, watching as many episodes of *Frasier* or *Sex and the City* as you can. When you need a change of pace, have a nap. It's tiring, all this self-care and relaxing. If you're all napped out, turn to your carefully selected stack of magazines and newspapers you've gathered for your hibernation weekend. We always wish we had time to read more. Well, this is the weekend for that. Indulge your literature fetish.

The big question is, should you have a partner in crime for your weekend in bed? I'll leave that for you to decide. Just slow down—by yourself or with a lover—and you'll see that there is nothing more restorative and mind settling than a whole weekend of nothing.

DON'T JUST TAKE IT FROM ME ...

"Sometimes, between traveling for work and family commitments, my boyfriend and I don't get to see each other on weekends. So we now actually schedule into our calendars one weekend every six weeks where we hide indoors, stay in bed, catch up, and you can guess what else. I think it's saved our relationship."

Fiona, 34, architect, Seattle

"I have times when I just want to wallow. I'm actually doing the world a favor by burying myself under my comforter all day long. And I emerge twenty-four hours later feeling right as rain again."

Rana, 29, teacher, Toronto

NO REGRETS

At least try to spend one day doing absolutely nothing. The apartment will always need cleaning, there'll always be people to see, but you won't always have the luxury of shutting yourself off and behaving so indulgently.

63 Learn to Speak the Truth, Even if It's Painful

Lying to those you love—or even to yourself—is a terrible shame, to say the least, and a disaster in most circumstances.

But it can be terribly hard to speak the truth and to speak it kindly.

If you want to sleep well at night, tell the truth. The more tangled the web you weave, the more you struggle to keep up with the inventions of your mind. Silly things will give you away: fidgeting on your seat, not being able to look people in the eye, covering your mouth as another lie slips out.

Why do people lie? My buddy does it to fill a gap in his knowledge—if he's feeling insecure or vulnerable, he makes something up to cover his weakness. It's such a shame. He's a great guy, and this is the one aspect of his personality that prevents others from being close with him.

I've had to tell the truth in difficult circumstances

before. At work once, I messed up a project, and I stood up and took the flak instead of letting my subordinates take the fall. I felt my bright light dim with the bosses for a few weeks, but I could sleep at night. And I believed, ultimately, that the people in charge knew I was someone who would stand up and be counted.

DON'T JUST TAKE IT FROM ME . . .

"The hardest lesson I've had to learn in life has a lot to do with being honest with yourself: some people will like you and others won't, no matter what you do or how decent you are. Don't manipulate your beliefs or character to try to win them over. Always speak the truth."

Bonnie, 40, homemaker, Hoboken, New Jersey

"I caught my husband in a massive lie about our financial situation a few years ago. It staggered me. It wasn't the problem that hurt me so much—it was the fact he hadn't told me the truth. My whole world fell apart because of a lie, and he is having to work hard to win back my faith in him. Lies aren't worth it."

Lynn, 36, homemaker, Santa Fe, New Mexico

IF YOU CAN'T LEARN TO SPEAK THE TRUTH . . .

Pipe down. Don't feel the need to chitchat away and get yourself into trouble. "It is better to offer no excuse than a bad one," said George Washington. And he's got a point. When you're tempted to twist the truth, just shut it.

64 Ride a Mechanical Bull

One of the easiest highs you can get in a bar isn't flashing your business or kissing the bartender. It's jumping onto a mechanical bull.

I'm going to let you in on a little secret: they are not as scary as they look. Sure, you get flung left and right, bounced up and down (wear a good bra), and shaken like a Polaroid picture, but nothing actually hurts. Even the inevitable crash landing isn't so bad—I promise your ego is all that will be bruised.

There's something fun and sexy about riding a bull. Remember serious Miranda letting it all out on a bull when the girls swapped sex in their usual city for sex in Los Angeles? It's a safe wild, a predictable scare, and the boys love watching it.

I rode my first bull—sober—at our work holiday party more than a year ago. Everyone was mingling and chatting while the huge beast stood still, like a big pink elephant no one would acknowledge in the middle of the room. The party was fine, but I wanted to get it going. So I set the night into action. The party turned from a refined, dull affair into a gathering of loud, fun clapping teammates as we all spurred on one another and downed shots for courage.

That night, fashion directors lost their composure as their shirts rode up, beauty editors failed to sit pretty, and the photo department struggled to capture more than ten seconds of riding time. But we were all addicted.

Whether you want to get a cheap thrill, a confidence boost, or the attention of the handsome guy at the bar, riding a mechanical bull is just the ticket. And if you fall off, it's like life—you just get back onto your feet, dust yourself off, and get straight back into the saddle. Yeehaw!

DON'T JUST TAKE IT FROM ME . . .

"I rode a mechanical bull—in a dress! I was impressed at how well I managed to ride the bull without a Britney Spears–esque moment, but I was *really* impressed by the girls who were petrified by the idea of riding the bull and then hopped on to conquer their fear."

Jen, 32, blogger, Los Angeles

"I'm not sure I'd ride a bull every week—the landing is a bit of a humiliating shock even though it doesn't physically hurt—but it's a sexy thing to do every now and again. It gets the adrenaline going . . . especially if you're aware of a sexy man watching you!"

Ali, 25, sales assistant, San Diego

IF YOU CAN'T RIDE A MECHANICAL BULL . . .

Find another bar-based dare that makes an evening go *bang*. Downing Flaming Drambuies (with fire extinguisher at hand) or giving your pals flirtation challenges will make any night fun.

65 Quit the Job You Hate

The shocking truth is that we spend more time at work with our colleagues than with our friends and family. Often leaving the office depleted and exhausted, we can do nothing but slump on the sofa in front of the television for the few remaining hours of the day. Now, if you're on a fast path to success, if you feel real passion for your industry, or if you love your team, your boss, and the office canteen, this could be worth it.

The minute you're not or you don't, you're in trouble.

You can moan about your sucky boss and your early-morning meetings forever—or you can quit and start again.

This sounds scary, I admit. We get kind of comfy in a place. It's a type of human resources–approved Stockholm syndrome, where we love and hate our captors in equal measure.

But you won't realize what a negative impact a bad job has on your whole life until you gather up your guts and take a chance.

A few years ago, I worked for the most influential newspaper in Great Britain. Everyone was impressed; I had a good salary and an incredible expense account. But after only six months, I was miserable. I deserved my salary—and the rest—for working long twelve-hour days. And the envious expense account was scarily explained away by the editor: "Well, working here, you never get to see your family and friends, so if you want to go for a blowout meal on the weekend with them, the company can cover it. Call it compensation to keep your loved ones sweet."

Everyone around me was gray. Their skin, their hair, their suits. An air of unenthusiastic reluctance hung over us all.

I had to get out.

I spent every spare moment of my commute time and weekends sending out my résumé and calling contacts. Thankfully, I got a job and my escape route became clear. I felt embarrassed that I had stuck it out only for a short time, but I didn't want to become like my poor colleagues, dejected and trapped, or develop nasty bullying techniques of my own, just to survive.

My family and friends were relieved—they'd seen a change in me in a short space of time and didn't like it.

We all have options. We all have inner resources that will spur us on. The human spirit is strong and resilient, and our fight for survival (financial, mental, physical) will kick in when we feel we've hit the end of the road.

So if you feel trapped, ask around, network, retrain, gain qualifications, and scour Web sites and newspapers for vacancies. You spend too much time at work for it to make you miserable.

DON'T JUST TAKE IT FROM ME . . .

"My boss victimized me for years. His behavior was so bad that eventually I called HR and said I wanted out. I signed away my bonus—everything! But I knew I had to get out. I did some soul-searching and came full circle. I had to leave to see what I still loved about my career, and I took those parts into a new job, with new light."

Suzy, 38, events marketer, New York City

"I quit my last job because I realized the owner of the company was a pompous, arrogant, dishonest, immoral asshole whom I didn't want to be associated with anymore. His company was all smoke and mirrors. It was scary, but I now am happier and healthier, have more time to myself, and make more money."

Leigh, 30, brand manager, Pittsburgh

IF YOU CAN'T QUIT THE JOB YOU HATE . . .

Take out your stress at the gym rather than at home. It's scary how quickly unsolved problems at work can turn into problems in your relationships. At the very least, scour the Web for job opportunities so you have a sense of what is out there.

66 Acknowledge Your Own Achievements

We are remarkably stingy when it comes to handing out compliments to the most important person in our lives: ourselves. We don't pat ourselves on the back very often. Why? Are we scared of bragging, showing off, getting too big for our britches? Or are we suffering from impostor syndrome? Are we worried that if we ever take a step back and congratulate ourselves, someone will tap us on the shoulder and say, "Er, excuse me, madam, you don't belong here. What do you think you are doing with this fab job/good salary/lovely husband/tiny waist?" We all have times like that, when we feel we don't deserve the good things that have come our way.

Well, guess what? We do!

You don't have to shout about your good fortune (it's not luck—you made it happen) from the rooftops. You just have to acknowledge it to yourself and be proud of your life so far.

When you connect with a new person, acknowledge your good social skills. When you run a half marathon, acknowledge your fitness level. When you submit a proposal at work, acknowledge your conscientiousness.

Treat yourself when you do something well or right or decent. Find the pleasure in simple things that make you feel valued and treasured. For me, it's a bubble bath a few nights a week with my phone switched off and a new magazine to devour. For others, it could be a massage or a half hour every morning to meditate or a new pair of shoes. Find little rewards to remind yourself just how great you are, how much you have achieved, and how the future is not a threat but a promise of new experiences.

Having this kind of integrity and respect for the person you are will help you to achieve even more of your goals, becoming an even more secure and confident person.

I used to suffer from impostor syndrome all the time. If someone commented on what a cool job I had, or what a nice accent, or what a great apartment,

I always looked for the counterbalance: "it's very stressful," or "I don't like it," or "it's too small." Now I graciously accept any compliment that comes my way and, as a silent nod to myself, agree with the giver.

Here is a good trick when you're feeling nervous about the future or how you've spent your time up until this point. Look back to the person you were ten years ago. What would that younger person have wanted for herself in the future: a job, a positive outlook on life, a workout routine, good friends, and a cool bar to hang out in? However vacuous or silly these may seem, jot them down. Now think about your reality. I bet you can tick most of these things off—and I bet you've surpassed your younger self's expectations, too.

When I'm feeling worried that I could get fired, or wondering how I'm going to pay my mortgage, or growing anxious that I will never, ever find a dream man, it's easy to doubt everything I've built up for myself. But looking at what I've achieved so far—not discounting the mistakes, because they are surely life lessons, too—gives me the strength to know I can handle the future with courage and with the support of my loved ones.

DON'T JUST TAKE IT FROM ME . . .

"The first time I can remember feeling good about myself was when I quit swimming. After fifteen years of swimming four, five hours a day, I thought about what I really wanted to do. And it wasn't that. I was worried about letting my parents down—but I'd got to the Olympic trials, and what more could I do? So I acknowledged all I'd done up till that point and thought, *How do I make my life even better?* I acknowledged my accomplishments and then moved on."

Bethany, 30, marketing manager, Pittsburgh, Pennsylvania

"It took meditation to make me slow down, stop panicking for the future, and bask in the glory of what I had already achieved. I was like a swinging monkey, always looking for the next branch to grip on to, never looking back before letting go. Meditation taught me that moving forward was good but that I should enjoy the motion of the swing, too, and that I needed to sometimes look behind me to see how far I'd come. I'm a much happier monkey now."

Melissa, 40, chef, Tulum, Mexico

IF YOU CAN'T ACKNOWLEDGE YOUR OWN ACHIEVEMENTS . . .

Be honest with your friends and family. Tell them you're feeling a bit down or like a failure, and get their feedback. Ask what they think your biggest achievement is so far. They will surely remember times and things that you've long forgotten, which will give you a renewed sense of pride and strength. And always congratulate your friends and family when they have achieved something remarkable, too. However confident someone may appear on the outside, compliments often provide a much-needed boost.

67 Laugh at Yourself

I am still haunted by something that happened to me at school when I was ten years old. I was in gym class, and we were running around playing tag. My shorts fell down, exposing my knickers. Now, really it was quite funny. I mean, I wasn't indecently exposing myself and luckily none of the boys had noticed, but I turned the color of a beet and sulked on the bleachers for the rest of the session.

The bullies noticed, of course. Sensing my embarrassment, they relished every second of my discomfort, telling the boy I had a crush on, laughing at me, and generally making my life a misery until a different girl had an unfortunate event that gave them an excuse to pick on someone new (some of the girls in my class really were nasty little things, looking back).

Now, if I could have had a chat with my ten-year-old self, I'd have said, *Laugh it off—who cares? Make a joke about flashing and carry on playing.* But instead I made a victim out of myself. If you can highlight your flaws and mishaps first, the power is taken away from anyone else to do so and you keep control.

Laughing at yourself means never taking yourself too seriously. Instead of becoming a joke, you'll be the joker, someone who is fun to be around.

Recently, for example, my friends and I were at a fabulous ball, looking rather elegant, I might add. A good friend took a tumble in her heels and stumbled (with her dress up round her waist) to the bottom of the stairs. We looked down, mortified for her, but we didn't get a chance to help. She got up quickly, shook herself down, said with a glint in her eye, "Sorry, girls, but you know I like to be the center of attention," and strutted off to the bar. Now, how sexy is that? Confident, strong, and funny. Thankfully, I'm more like that now myself.

DON'T JUST TAKE IT FROM ME . . .

"If you don't laugh at yourself, you internalize and agonize over everything. If you have a good foundation, hopefully you will have the confidence to run with whatever life throws at you. The brain controls everything, so if you can train yourself to think happy thoughts, even in silly moments, positive things come your way. I've made a fool of myself so often. Failure is a good teacher. So falling off a bike is okay. Just laugh."

Wright, 38, floor designer, Tuscaloosa, Alabama

"In the Bible, Proverbs 17:22 is about how a merry heart restores and fulfills the soul. I think negative feelings get in the way of being creative. It's human nature to be negative—and one negative thought can feed another one. So try to look on the bright side and laugh. I've learned recently that if you deal with a negative thought immediately, it doesn't have the chance to have a life. You release it and let it go. Learn, then smile."

Caroline, 56, cake-company owner, Annapolis

Don't get too hurt when other people have a giggle at your expense—bite your tongue. And certainly don't laugh at other people! Those in glass houses shouldn't throw stones, as a little bird used to say.

68 Learn to Meditate

Meditation had always seemed like hocus-pocus to me, a bit like an adult nap masquerading as something special. Yet more and more of my friends were being helped and rebuilt through meditation, so I started giving it some serious consideration.

When one of my idols, the inspirational Oprah, started discussing its merits, I knew I had to give it a try, but I was still a little reluctant. Then when I read *Eat, Pray, Love* for the first time and learned how Elizabeth Gilbert had managed to ignore a thousand mosquito bites (something I suffer from every time I venture somewhere tropical) while in a meditative state, I knew that to stop itching and scratching away at my own calmness, I had to give it a go *immediately*. So after yoga sessions, I would lie down and allow thoughts to float in and out of my head. I'd breathe deeply and rhythmically—in and out to the beat of four—and feel the life within my body and the energy that I created just outside it. It wasn't hard to get there. It's amazing how much time we waste, stressing ourselves out with unnecessary noise—turning on the television and the radio unconsciously, calling friends while we're in the bath, answering e-mails or reading a newspaper while we're eating. Are we scared of being alone with our own thoughts? Perhaps, but until you stop to feel your body and allow your thoughts to flow freely, you will never know your true power and potential. Try it.

Get comfortable first—you don't want distracting thoughts of aching knees or a numb bum to disturb you (but you don't need to sit in the lotus position— do whatever feels right). Be silent. Close your eyes. Focus on taking deep chest-expanding breaths in and out of the nose. If you do nothing else, just concentrate on your breathing. If worrying thoughts or stressful feelings pop into your head, return to your breathing.

Meditating isn't hard, and it invigorates you like nothing else. Fresh ideas will suddenly arrive in your head from nowhere, as will solutions to previously unfathomable problems. Go on. Give it a go.

DON'T JUST TAKE IT FROM ME . . .

"Meditation is the simplest method of energy boosting you can imagine. And it's so transportable. You can do it anywhere, anytime, to get a clearer perspective on anything. Even when I'm in a taxi and we get stuck in traffic, I close my eyes and meditate. In the past, I would have got stressed and sworn at the driver. Now I just accept it and use the time to chill out."

Winnie, 29, actor, Hamilton, Bermuda

"My boyfriend laughs at me for getting out of bed early and sitting on a hard floor every morning to meditate. Especially on the cold mornings! But just taking that time for myself is invaluable. And he'd be a lot calmer if he tried it!"

Amy, 24, waitress, Las Vegas, Nevada

IF YOU CAN'T LEARN TO MEDITATE . . .

At least learn to be quiet for a while. When you get up in the morning or arrive home at night and you're tempted to put the television or radio on or to call a friend on the phone, don't. Let your mind enjoy some peace and quiet.

69 Do Something that Scares You

When you think *scary,* what do you imagine? Freddy Krueger? Bungee jumping? Sarah Palin? Truly scary things can be seemingly simple tasks that require courage and determination to achieve. And with each challenging task you complete, your soul strengthens and you feel brave. This helps you to further pursue your goals and take wider strides to becoming a fully competent, confident you. The true importance of doing things that are scary hit me last year when I ended things with a boyfriend. I had built my life around him and pushed friends, hobbies, and personal well-being to the side. Being suddenly alone was scary—but amazingly, a few days into my new life as a single woman, I felt bolstered by my courage and control. I realized I felt alive. My life was my own and

I was in charge—I could do anything. I decided to do something that scared me more often—if possible, every day.

I went to the cinema on my own for the first time, I got a Brazilian wax, I went naked in a steam room, I went on live television, and I started wearing flip-flops (something I'd put off for years because friends said they hurt between your toes before you got used to them). I even flew to Austin, Texas, for a weekend of exploring on my own because no one else wanted to. Suddenly, my eyes—and horizons—were open. Why had I lived such a small, miserable life for so long? Throughout my thirty-one years I had been ruled by the fear of what people would think of me, or the fear of my own body, or the fear of my limitations.

The more you do, the more you go for it and the more you have to gain. As one incredibly brave woman, Helen Keller—who was surely scared every day by obstacles thrown her way—said, "Life is either a daring adventure—or nothing!" Be brave and be strong. Things will stop being so scary and start being exhilarating chances to grab life with two hands.

DON'T JUST TAKE IT FROM ME . . .

"Doing extreme sports like paragliding and surfing led me to find an inner strength and daredevil streak at the grand old age of thirty-three. Now I'm not the girl who wimps out of things or always says no. In every aspect of my life, I take the challenge and say yes. It's made me feel much freer and happier—even when the scary thing is something such as asking my boss for a pay raise."

Jacqui, 35, waitress, Philadelphia

NO REGRETS

"A dating coach told me the only way I was going to have a healthier self-image—and eventually a healthy relationship—was to be brave: if I saw a man I liked the look of in a coffee shop, I should smile. A smile is a small thing, but it takes guts. I've tried it a few times, and the worst thing that can happen is that he doesn't smile back. Try leaving your comfort zone every now and then."

Sandra, 28, student, San Diego

IF YOU CAN'T DO SOMETHING THAT SCARES YOU . . .

Read autobiographies of great thinkers and leaders, such as Barack Obama and Sir Richard Branson, who were brave enough to do scary things and change the world. Their tales will bring you encouragement—and perhaps a new way of thinking.

70 Become a Bit of a Hippie

Doing a little incense sniffing and caftan wearing can be good for the soul. The modern day hippie isn't smelly or a druggie and certainly doesn't remove her pants at the first hint of an orgy. She is much more about free love in the "please don't destroy the environment or my karma" kind of way, and that's very important to remember.

As a teenager, after my strange goth phase, I went through the requisite chilled-out phase—I had a thing for Day-Glo and plastic beads, and I would wear flowers in my hair and paint my lids with blue eye shadow at any given opportunity. Being a hippie seemed daring and different—despite my whole class trying to be hippies at the same time (an irony lost on me).

I remember huddling in a friend's kitchen when I was fourteen, desperately trying to light on fire a slightly moldy banana skin, having been told of its hallucinogenic qualities by her older brother. We didn't get high, but the smoke alarm went off and I was grounded for a week when all the parents figured out what we'd been trying to do.

In the years following that, if given the opportunity to sit under a tree with a long-haired guitarist who had a penchant for Bob Dylan, I was in heaven. Love, peace, and understanding. That's what life was all about.

Until I hit twenty-one.

I stopped caring so much about the world at large and became more greedy, cynical, and industrious. I no longer searched for hippies; I searched for mentors who could inspire me to get to the top. Flowers— pah, I laughed in the face of flowers. I wanted a power suit with twelve-inch shoulder pads and I wanted it yesterday.

At twenty-two, I bought a house, bought a car, and flew around the world to a series of glamorous destinations. My carbon footprint went from a ballet slipper to a full-on clown shoe.

My friends were the same. We were less supportive of one another and our communities and more driven to beat thy neighbor and get rich quick.

Now in my thirties, I've mellowed out a bit and realized what is more important than money and my profession: friends, family, true love, and self-respect. I know my chakra is green and I should take off my shoes more and walk barefoot through grass. I know acupuncture can work. I understand that "five fruits and vegetables a day" is the minimum and we should all try to eat more from the land in an organic, sustainable way.

Stepping off the hamster wheel to understand yourself can really make for a stronger, healthier you.

So find yourself a Reiki healer to improve your energy flow or escape to a farm run by holistic practitioners to pull you through a tough winter. Instead of heading to a bar, head to the spa with your girlfriends and relax in the peace and quiet with a massage therapist and an open mind. And when you see someone who seems particularly calm and resilient, ask what his or her secret is. This is a wonderful way to live. Right on, dudes!

DON'T JUST TAKE IT FROM ME . . .

"I left my job and became a freelance charity adviser, which gave me the free time to start a course in hypnotherapy and helped me not get so stressed commuting or upset by office politics. I met like-minded people who wanted to help others and enjoyed simple things in life, like walking on a beach or admiring a beautiful painting. My health—and my heart—is much better now!"
Julia, 37, charity worker, London

"My boyfriend had just ended our relationship and I was devastated. My friends were planning their own weddings and futures and I was lonely and depressed, so I booked a two-week yoga retreat in Goa, where I did nothing but drink herbal tea and do

downward dogs. The instructors there taught me to honor myself and my body—physically and spiritually. It was an amazing
time for me."

Leah, 28, personal trainer, Santa Fe, New Mexico

IF YOU CAN'T BECOME A HIPPIE . . .

Educate yourself with their teachings instead. Take
the phone off the hook for the weekend, stock up on
chamomile tea and aromatherapy candles, and read a
few good books. I recommend *The Road Less Traveled*
by M. Scott Peck for day and *The Tao of Pooh* by
Benjamin Hoff for bedtime.

71 Date Outside Your Type

A wise friend said to me once, "You might like Mars
bars at the moment, but you might not like them in
ten years! And how do you know they're your favorite
thing in the candy store?"

Too often we fall in love with a type or simply because the man in question falls in love with us. We
don't think about who and what will suit us in twenty-
five years' time. Hell, we don't think about who'll suit
us next year.

So experiment. I don't mean sexually, although of
course you don't know what you like till you've tried
it. I'm talking romantically.

Say yes to the guy who stops you in the coffee shop,
even though you don't know much about him. Accept

an offer from the bookish type, even if you're usually drawn to jocks. Think you hate actors? Give one a shot if he asks. He might not be your usual, but you can't judge a book by its cover, so why try. And don't just stop at the type of men you date; try new types of dates, too. A meal for two followed by a trip to the cinema is safe but boring. Venture out of town, or try a play or a new activity. Anyone can appear entertaining for an hour over dinner or silent during a film. A different style of date will push you into seeing things differently.

There are all sorts of men out there, so don't cut yourself off. Even if on first glance you think he's wrong, if something at all sparks your interest, say yes! Go on, I dare you. Take a chance . . .

DON'T JUST TAKE IT FROM ME . . .

"Date a variety of people: actor, athlete, bartender, chef, cowboy, DJ, doctor, firefighter, lawyer, model, musician, pilot, politician, publicist, restaurant/nightclub owner, sports agent, teacher, writer. You will appreciate more the person you marry and what he does (or does not do) for a living. I have most of them down, so I can probably pick one and get married now, right?"
Rhiannon, 29, sports writer, Miami

"I always thought I'd end up with someone older, richer, and taller than me, and I certainly dated a lot of men just like that. But somehow along the way, the one who grabbed my attention was a dude two inches shorter than me, four years younger than me, and a struggling artist. Yet without a doubt, he's the one. We're getting married next year, and my former relationship qualifiers just seem ridiculous now!"
Georgina, 36, chef, Austin, Texas

At least gossip with your girlfriends to get a real feel of the wider man market so you don't look back in fifty years' time and think, *Oh, shucks—I was so narrow-minded!*

72 Be One of the Guys

Being a girl is a fabulous thing, but sometimes we need to hang out with the lads to take things down a notch. We ladies can get a bit gossipy and hysterical at times, so playing things cool with some male company acts as a decompressor.

I'm not talking about being one of the guys just to snag one of them. That's one of my pet peeves, in fact: those girls who pretend they love baseball and drinking beer just to impress the men and get a drunken kiss at the end of a night in a bar. No, this is about spending time with men for friendship's sake. It's for trying new things and really seeing men in their natural habitat: with other guys, drinking beer, talking sports—and being surprisingly lovely about the women in their lives (especially their moms).

I'm a real girl's girl. I love women—I love getting to know what makes them tick and figuring out how I can encourage them and learn from them. But growing up with two little brothers in a house filled with their friends, I had to learn to find farting funny from an early age. It's been great training. Nothing shocks me. Men are naturally more prone to enjoy a few things in life that prudish women find shocking: toilet humor, copious amounts of beer, Hooters waitresses, and basketball stars' salaries. Being around the guys not only helps you to understand this (a skill that you can take into romantic relationships with the opposite sex), it also helps you to chill out. And you'll soon be able to decipher between what is downright bad in life and what is just a little bit cheeky.

DON'T JUST TAKE IT FROM ME . . .

"I have an obsession with soccer—and David Beckham in particular—which my girlfriends refuse to indulge but my guy friends love me for. I actually know about the offside rule. I'm now included on their trips to the games on Saturdays, which is much more fun than trawling malls with girls moaning about the size of their bottoms."

Gina, 27, waitress, Los Angeles

"Men have a matter-of-fact approach to life that I learned to value during my last relationship crisis. Being men, my friends knew what my ex-boyfriend's behavior meant, they were actually able to say to me, 'You need to be with someone who makes you a priority, not an option.' My relationship wasn't going anywhere, and they offered the male perspective that I needed."

Caroline, 30, personal trainer,
Sacramento, California

FREE SPIRIT

Encourage your girlfriends to open their eyes to some male pursuits—there really is something fun about chicken wings and beer on the couch on a rainy Sunday afternoon. Men are good at chilling out. Bring that skill to your girlfriends.

73 Eat an Exotic Meat

Alligator sandwich? Kangaroo kebab? Shark curry? Okay, so I know what you're thinking: what's wrong with a piece of cod or a turkey club sandwich? Well, nothing. But sometimes, especially when you are traveling, it's gutsy to experiment in the gourmet department.

I'm all about trying anything once. How can you have an opinion on something if you don't know what you are talking about? I'd stop at monkey-brain soup (a delicacy in many a foreign country), but apart from that, a nibble here and there will make you look like a good sport, a good-natured traveler, and a game-for-a-laugh kind of gal. I ate piranha in Peru—I didn't see the fuss. And elk in Colorado—it was quite tasty. I ate a pigeon once by mistake at a hotel restaurant in the English countryside and was delighted with its tenderness.

So spice things up and tickle your taste buds. You don't know what you know until you know it.

DON'T JUST TAKE IT FROM ME . . .

"Many of my vacations have become defined not by what I saw but what I ate. Every culture offers such a diverse range of tastes and textures. Most of my vacation albums have countless photos of me enjoying local delicacies in different locales—normally with the local specialty cocktail in my hand. Food is such a part of a place that I can't be snooty and turn my nose up at anything."

Sandra, 35, charity volunteer, Los Angeles

"I was enjoying a piece of deer once at a friend's wedding when I came across some shot—a bit of bullet. I found this rather disturbing, as did my fillings, but the groom said it was good luck, so I went with it. I'll never forget that dinner."

Katie, 29, writer, Brooklyn

IF YOU CAN'T GET AN EXOTIC MEAT . . .

Try other exotic foods instead. An olive is not just an olive, for example. Every different region in which they are grown pickles them differently and stuffs them with various delights. And don't close off your palate just because you're a vegetarian. Experiment.

74 Play Hooky

Life shouldn't be all work, work, work. Sometimes it needs to be more about play. So what do you do if you've eaten up your vacation allowance but fancy a duvet day? You cheat.

There are a few rules to follow to play hooky with minimum disruption to your team, your boss, and your standing in the office.

Don't plan any big meetings for the day you're going to stay away. Having to cancel stuff will highlight your absence, and more questions will be asked. Don't do it more than once or twice a year. Playing hooky is a rare treat, not a God-given right. And if you're playing hooky because you're planning a big drunken night out on the town and suspect you may feel worse for wear the next day, keep your social calendar to yourself. Alarm bells will ring the minute you don't show up.

Start coughing or sneezing in the office in the run-up to your MIA day. Don't get too theatrical, but just plant a few subtle seeds that something nasty is going around. Put in a few hours' extra work leading up to the big day. Don't leave piles of work for others to do. They'll resent you and your mysterious illness. Tell one trusted colleague what you are doing (but don't play hooky with a co-worker). Having a reliable partner in crime can help you cover your tracks and pick up any urgent workload.

Lastly, enjoy it! If you're going to do this risky business, make it count. Go somewhere fun—or plan a fantastic day of hibernation complete with a fridge full of treats and a TiVo full of your favorite shows.

DON'T JUST TAKE IT FROM ME . . .

"When I first started dating my boyfriend, I couldn't bear to be away from him. Luckily, he felt the same way. One day, we just couldn't stand to be pulled apart, so we took the day off together. We didn't do anything much. Well, you can imagine what we did—it was a new relationship! But the naughty backstory made us like giggly schoolkids again and bonded us even further."

Monica, 33, human-resources assistant,
Philadelphia, Pennsylvania

"My boss is terrible at letting people have their vacations. He always finds issues with them, even though we work hard and put in really long hours. He's a workaholic and wants us to do the same. For years I followed his example, until I started getting ill and my family noticed a change in me. Now, when I feel it's all getting to be too much, I take a day off and head to a double screening at the cinema, where I can turn off my phone. He knows what I'm up to, but what can he say?"

Clara, 31, public-relations executive, New York City

IF YOU CAN'T PLAY HOOKY . . .

At least use your lunch breaks wisely. Don't be a slave to your desk. The sad truth is that workers don't always get thanks or praise for putting in extra hours and effort. Work hard when it counts, but then on a quiet day, book a lunch with a friend or go to the gym for an hour. And don't be afraid to be the first to leave the office in the evening. If your work is done, get out and enjoy your life. All work and no play makes you a very dull person.

FREE SPIRIT

CHIC GEEK

75 Learn Quotes from Grease

An instant bond can be created with people all over the world by repeating a few words first uttered by John Travolta and his T-bird pals or Olivia Newton-John and the Pink Ladies in *Grease,* the most amazingly quotable movie of all time. I'm not pretending any of the words resonate as importantly as a speech by Hillary Clinton on the health-care system, but for a certain gender and age group, these words were pretty darn influential.

I use lines from the movie without thinking about it. Honestly, to me they are as powerful as something uttered by Benjamin Franklin in the eighteenth century. I would argue they have shaped America's youth just as greatly, and Olivia Newton-John was certainly easier to look at. Who didn't want to burst through the doors of her school on the last day of the year singing "We Go Together" with great abandon and munching on cotton candy?

Grease shaped our ideas of summers, summer romances, school romances, and our school days. We walked around playgrounds saying, "That's my name—don't wear it out," when an annoying person called. Or we said we felt "like a defective typewriter," not realizing that meant we'd skipped a period and could be pregnant. My friends and I have plundered the script for jokes and catchphrases since I can remember. And even now, in our thirties, a sly reference will always draw a pat on the back.

The one danger, of course, is that you use a quote, continue to say the entire scene, and then just want to rush home and watch the whole movie.

And sure, experiment with *Grease 2,* but quoting the follow-up is not for *Grease* purists. We are better than that. And besides—can you ever remember a line from a sequel?

When it comes to filling time, bonding with friends, and making serious points lightly, it's true: *Grease* really is the word.

DON'T JUST TAKE IT FROM ME . . .

"I wanted to be Olivia Newton-John so badly when I was younger. I loved that she could do good girl and bad girl just as well. I first discovered *Grease* at the same time I was obsessed with the Jem dolls—you know, those truly outrageous rock-star figures. Jem was the same, good and bad. And I think I've been a bit like that ever since. A straight-laced geek in the office and a party girl at night."

Karrie, 32, office manager, Brooklyn

"For about ten birthdays in a row, I insisted my parents let me throw a slumber party like the one the Pink Ladies had at Frenchy's house in the film. Unfortunately, no boys made Romeo-like maneuvers on the front drive and we didn't go shooting down any drainpipes—but we loved singing and dancing in our pajamas."

Tiffany, 26, student, Providence, Rhode Island

It's not quite as good, but if you can't get with *Grease,* try *Dirty Dancing* instead. I don't know how often you'll be able to use the "I carried a watermelon" line, but others from the movie have come in handy in my life. "No one puts Baby in a corner" is good when a friend won't join you on the dance floor. "I'll do your hair for you, baby, make you look pretty" works when a friend needs a bit of a cuddle but you're trying to play it down.

76 Read the Book Before You See the Film

Some filmmakers do great jobs of interpreting your dreams and an author's imagination onto the big screen. But sadly, many don't. That's why I advise you to read the book before seeing the movie. A dodgy two hours in the cinema could ruin forever a novel you could have loved for life.

Some films are better than the books: *Bridget Jones's Diary,* for example. The book was fun; the film was classic comedy. And no one is going to sigh and tell you off for not picking it up off the bookshelf instead of renting the DVD.

Other recent adaptations of good books have been beautifully acted and well crafted, but they still lack all the delicacies that a book allows you to add.

An author has no budget or time constraint, and of course neither does your imagination. Film producers have to battle with both these things, plus they have the weight on their shoulders of making something beloved to many.

The Other Boleyn Girl was a great historical romp; as a book, it was sexy, educational, and scary, quite a feat for the author, Philippa Gregory. The film was just wrong. Natalie Portman as Anne Boleyn? *No!* She was concentrating so hard on her English accent, she forgot she was playing a woman so charismatic that the King of England abandoned his wife and the Catholic Church to have her.

As soon as you've seen a film, your visual memory is set. Even if you enjoy the condensed Hollywood version so much that you rush straight out to the bookshop to indulge in the tale for a second time, it will never be the same. The actors are the characters. I mean, can you imagine reading Ian Fleming's James Bond novels now? They are supposed to be fabulous, but without Daniel Craig in tight blue swimming trunks, what's the point? That's all you'll be thinking of, anyway.

DON'T JUST TAKE IT FROM ME . . .

"As a real Harry Potter obsessive, I nervously awaited the first movie. These characters were larger than life and I was so worried that a huge studio would Americanize them—and soon Harry would have a Los Angeles accent, huge white teeth, and a tattoo. Thankfully, they kept to the principles—and a British cast—and the first time Harry ventured into Diagon Alley, I cried because it was so perfect."

Andrea, 32, brand manager, London

"The Golden Compass was my vacation-reading treat last year. I escaped into the world of Oxford, dæmons, and big battles in the sky. But I was a bit slow off the mark and reading it only starting when the film was already out and getting a lot of buzz. I could see how the actors got cast, but I was glad I invested my time in the book before I finally saw the movie."

Jill, 32, software architect, Los Angeles

IF YOU CAN'T READ THE BOOK BEFORE YOU SEE THE FILM . . .

Read the book after you've seen the movie—if you enjoyed it! Don't miss out on a great reading experience just because you've already seen it done on the big screen. You may know the finale, but you will find subtle nuances and delights that a filmmaker just wouldn't have the time to embrace.

77 Keep a Camera with You at All Times

As I write, I'm sitting in a Starbucks. I had to get out of my apartment. My deadlines had imprisoned me in a world of no human interaction, and getting out to a coffee shop was the answer. Besides, I need the caffeine and the excuse to get washed and dressed. And even on this rainy day in a Starbucks, there are moments happening, moments worth capturing.

Next to me there's a Polish family, with a little

blond boy singing and playing drums on his organic apple-juice carton while his proud grandfather hums along, grinning from ear to ear.

A herd of cyclists races in to get some bottles of water.

A little family of ducklings enter. Four children, in matching yellow raincoats with the hoods up and navy plastic boots protecting their toes, quack about milk shakes and black and white cookies.

Then there's the subtle eye contact between some of the patrons. This is a famously hot pickup joint, so dolled-up single women line the tables near the entrance, pretending to focus on their *New York Post* while sizing up every man who enters. The guys stumble in after rain-soaked jogs, casual in sweats and baseball caps, clearly appreciative of the effort the ladies have made.

And this is all in five minutes in a coffee shop.

Often, we don't spend enough time looking around us, seeing the love and humor in everyday things. A camera can help us do that. Looking through a lens creates a barrier that makes it more acceptable to stare and admire.

The day I moved to New York, I decided to always keep a camera in my bag, and the best images haven't been the posed shots of friends on a night out. I've captured children jumping barefoot in the water from a burst fire hydrant. I've hit the right moment to snap a sunset between the skyscrapers of Thirty-second Street. I've caught a visitor's confusion at the roller skaters in Central Park.

Digital cameras are so reasonably priced now. Get a lightweight camera and throw it into your bag as you would your phone or wallet.

We don't think we'll forget the small moments of our lives, but we do. Our recollections fade with time. But photos don't. Get snapping.

DON'T JUST TAKE IT FROM ME . . .

"When I had my first child, I couldn't imagine her growing up and getting bigger. I certainly couldn't imagine her in a school uniform. But my mother warned me about how babies grow up fast, so I made sure my husband captured everything. We always had a camera on us because the best shots are always the unexpected moments. I'm glad we did. Now I look back at images and can't believe she was ever that small."

Abby, 34, homemaker, Tucson, Arizona

"I've broken a few cameras—carrying them with you at all times does cause damage. But I've always made replacing a camera my priority. I see photos as the cheapest form of entertainment. I can lose myself in old albums for hours. Looking at pictures is a great de-stressor and memory provoker. Some of my best photos are of small, inconsequential things: a fancily iced cake, a blooming flower, an autumn street. But they represent real beauty and remind me to keep my eyes open to life and possibility."

Erin, 32, photographer, Montreal

IF YOU CAN'T KEEP A CAMERA WITH YOU AT ALL TIMES . . .

At least make sure you develop and store the photos you do take. If you're more of a special-occasion snapper, fine, but your memory card is not a photo album.

Set yourself a rule: as soon as your card hits a certain number, print out the photos and also save them on a CD. It's worth the investment.

78 Find a Mentor

Life can be tough, so a few encouraging words from people that have trodden the path in front of you can make all the difference. The knowledge of someone who has been there and done that can turn a crazy, helpless situation into something you'll wear like a badge of honor. A mentor can show you the way.

I work in journalism, a highly competitive field where the good guys really stand out. I love writers and editors as a group, I really do—they are interesting, interested, and great storytellers. But the further up the ladder I've climbed, the lonelier it's become.

When I first took the job of editor in chief, I wanted to protect my team and resist moaning to my bosses, so I kept to myself and took on everyone else's problems along with my own.

Then someone asked, "Who do you go to for advice? Who's looking after you?" and I, for once, was dumbstruck. I had no one. So I put myself out there and befriended a great bloke who was the editor of a newspaper in Manhattan and a charming woman who had just been made the editor in chief of a glossy monthly.

I e-mailed them, they kindly replied, and soon lunches and dinners full of shared dilemmas, helpful advice, and encouraging good humor were abundant.

I didn't realize how much I needed someone in the industry to look up to until I found them. I was lucky. But choosing a mentor is a tricky business.

The first rule of thumb is to make sure she or he is not in competition with you. She should be secure, confident, and settled in what she is doing and who she is. The second rule is to pick someone discreet. If you're asking how to deal with your difficult boss or you're wondering if you should take that other job, you don't need your mentor sharing this information with anyone else. She should be a sounding board and a tower of strength—not a town crier. The minute you hear anything you've said to your mentor in a private conversation repeated to you by someone else, get out.

Thirdly, do know that mentoring has its time and place and that eventually you might outgrow each other. Mentoring can be exhausting. Don't use your mentor as a general therapist. Discuss your career path; don't bore her with questions about your annoying boyfriend.

Pay your mentor with cups of coffee and by taking her advice. If you've chosen the right one, she has years filled with failures, flops, and successes that you can learn from. If you continually choose to do the opposite of what she suggests, what's the point?

DON'T JUST TAKE IT FROM ME . . .

"I'm very confident at work, but when it comes to asking for a pay raise, for some reason I'm pathetic. My mentor made me see clearly and unabashedly what I was worth. He outlined my position and its value at other companies. He reminded me of my accomplishments and helped me understand what I'd learned from my failures. With a few months of discussion, I was strong enough to go to my boss and justify a higher wage. It worked, and every time I get my paycheck, I send my mentor an imaginary high five."

Joely, 27, beauty therapist, New Haven,
Connecticut

"Charles Dickens once wrote, 'Treasure the one who lightens the burden on anyone else.' And I really treasure my mentor, who I think stopped me from going mad when I was caught in a bitter power struggle at work. It's amazing how office politics can drag you down and force you to take your eye off the proper ball: producing good results. My mentor gave me advice on how to handle the bullies and focus on my own long-term goals."

Janice, 41, administrator, New Orleans,
Louisiana

IF YOU CAN'T FIND A MENTOR . . .

You may already have one. It may be your father, your best friend, or even one of your former schoolteachers. Once you recognize her and show your appreciation, you may be able to turn her into a real mentor. "We must find the time to stop and thank the people who make a difference in our lives," said Robert Kennedy, and I agree. And when you do stop and express gratitude for good advice, mentors want to help you even more.

79 Be a Mentor

When people ask me what the best thing is about my job, I answer without hesitation: seeing my team learn and grow. I oversee about sixty people, and nothing gives me more joy or fulfillment than seeing one of them earn a promotion, get excited about a project, or pull off a difficult task.

As long as people are team players, hard workers, and good at what they do, I will mentor them to within an inch of their lives. Even if they leave, I still feel an immense sense of pride when I see them pop up on television or on the masthead of a different magazine.

To be a good mentor, you have to eradicate any jealousy from your system. You can't be looking out for someone else's best interests when there's a little bitterness or resentment niggling away at you.

If my mentoring can encourage even one young person to get to the top of the field without being a competitive, paranoid weirdo (as so many journalists are), I'll have done my mentoring job.

We all have the power to teach. Indeed, as one of the greatest teachers of all time, Socrates, said, "You are not only good yourself, but the cause of goodness in others." I like that idea and have decided to live by it.

DON'T JUST TAKE IT FROM ME . . .

"I was a great swimmer as a teen, but an injury forced me to quit. Rather than becoming bitter and twisted by the whole thing, I took on the mentoring of the younger kids, and amazingly, I've relished their victories as much as I relished my own."

Beth, 30, consultant, Sarasota

"In school we had a system where the older kids would all take new kids under their wings, show them around, and protect them from bullies. That training must have stuck with me, because I'm still a real carer and nurturer. My role in human resources has allowed me to really encourage the new hires to take courses, learn to manage their managers, and think about their career progression and future goals."

Clara, 34, human-resources manager,
New York City

IF YOU CAN'T BE A MENTOR . . .

Give something back, somewhere. A good friend of mine helps out on weekends in homeless shelters in New York. It's an amazing thing to do, and what is even more amazing is that she gets just as much out of it as the people she helps. The mental and emotional reward of helping people younger or less fortunate than you is limitless.

80 Learn a Foreign Language

In all areas of life, communication is key—with your parents, your boyfriend, your boss, and the rest of the world.

As an eleven-year-old in the United Kingdom, I was given two foreign-language choices: French or German. I chose French because I quite liked old Brigitte Bardot movies at the time. French was considered the more difficult of the two, but my friends all went for it as well, and before long we were *zut alors*-ing our little socks off.

The highlight of learning a language as a student was the infamous trips abroad. When our time finally came at age fourteen, my friends and I were beyond excited. I'd been going to Paris to live with a French family for a few summers by then, but going with my English school buddies was going to be quite a different matter. As soon as we landed on French soil, we rushed into a café to order something we'd all fantasized about in our last textbook: *"une diabolo menthe et un croque monsieur, s'il vous plaît."* Translated, it turned out to be a rather unexciting glass of putrid green liquid that tasted like mouthwash and a toasted ham and cheese sandwich. But we loved it anyway because we were in Le Touquet and the waitress had understood us when we ordered.

Learning to speak a foreign language isn't just great

for ordering local culinary letdowns. Having knowledge of a language outside your own really does open up a new world to you. It is difficult—and the longer you leave it, the harder it gets (small children have brains like sponges for new words, so remember that if you have your own babies!)—but it is useful and fun. It allows you to geekily throw in vocabulary for your own amusement and to flex your mental muscles. It means you can go for date night to those kooky little independent cinemas where they show worthy foreign films and impress your new beloved by pointing out mistakes in the translated subtitles on the screen.

Encourage a friend to go to night school with you, or download language-lesson podcasts onto your iPod for your commute. The best way to learn is to actually get to where the language is spoken—just make sure you don't hang out with people who will talk to you in your mother tongue.

DON'T JUST TAKE IT FROM ME . . .

"I didn't realize how lucky I was to be brought up speaking two languages—English and Spanish—until I got to high school and all my friends were struggling to make their grades. Since then, I've appreciated both cultures of my parents and make a concerted effort to speak to my cousins in whichever language they use most. My friends are always very impressed, and it's proved useful at work, too."
Clara, 25, shop assistant, Dallas, Texas

"My husband and I are coming to it a little late, some would say, but when we retired, we bought a house in Spain and decided it was ridiculous not to be able to communicate with the women in the supermarket. So we attend night school and listen to those tapes, and although we'll never be scholars, I can confidently order a taxi and haggle with market stallholders now."

Helen, 55, homemaker, London

IF YOU CAN'T LEARN A FOREIGN LANGUAGE . . .

Memorize a few words and phrases that will be useful when you're traveling. *Please, thank you, hello, goodbye, yes, no* . . . these are the basics. And a good guidebook should have a few more, too. Just making that small amount of effort will please the locals and probably get you better service with a smile.

81 Keep a Diary

Now, this was a difficult one to decide whether to include. You see, I've had a few problems with diaries in the past.

I started my first diary when I was a teenager; I used it to moan about my mother. I'd scrawl some adolescent rant about how she was a bossy cow and I'd feel much better. Our nosy old bag of a cleaning lady found it, though (hidden under my bed), read it, and then passed it over to my mother. How disloyal and trouble hungry was she? I was grounded and Daisy was thanked. Life sucked.

Another time, a few years after I *didn't* learn my lesson, I left my diary vulnerable to nosy parkers again.

This time it was a friend, who spotted my entry about my first true crush and told him. I was mortified and wondered why I always felt the need to commit everything to paper.

But a few years (and a padlock) later, I do feel diaries are important things to keep. Not only are they useful for plotting relationship highs and lows—when you could be tempted to rose-tint things—and remembering what time of year you went on vacation, they are great at helping you recall magic moments. They can also remind you how you've survived tougher times than what you're going through currently.

Diaries do not have to be great works of literature. Some friends throw in mantras of the day or a new quote they've learned that speaks to them. Others use theirs as a form of therapy, where they can spill their innermost feelings and thoughts.

I keep the most basic of diaries, a paper desk diary, in which no one else would be able to make sense of my scrawls. I go back after each day and fill in highlights, unexpected meetings, parties, and so on. It's always fun to flip back to the same day the year before and see what I was doing then and what has changed.

A diary is a great way to keep your life on track and to congratulate yourself on how much you've achieved already.

DON'T JUST TAKE IT FROM ME . . .

"I went to a hypnotherapy course where they encouraged us to keep a diary. It was a mood diary, and we were taught to think beyond basic thoughts and deeds toward feelings and senses. It helped me to connect with myself, and I still keep a mood diary today. It's helped me to see the link between my feelings and my menstrual cycle, which has stopped me from thinking I'm mad."

Dana, 28, teacher, Hoboken

"I've been keeping diaries since I was a teenager, with the hope of one day passing them down to a daughter of my own. As a teen, my mother and I had terrible communications issues—she couldn't relate to me and I couldn't open up to her. I am so scared that could happen to me that I'm hoping by rereading and sharing my own diaries, I'll be able to remember what being young is like—and help my future daughter to understand that I was like her once, too."

Hilary, 35, event planner, Queens

IF YOU CAN'T KEEP A DIARY . . .

Set up a folder on your computer where you can store meaningful and relevant e-mails between you and good friends. If you've had a particularly hilarious night out, you know the banter the next day will be priceless. Save these messages for a rainy day to remind you of good times.

82 Embrace Your Naughty Side

Some of us find it hard to embrace our naughty nature—but we all have one.

Life does get more serious the older we get, and doing something silly or pointless can seem like a waste of time. There's always serious, worthy stuff to be doing: reading, writing, getting fit, or learning a new sport. But the more serious life gets, the more important it is to have fun—and the easiest way to have fun as an adult is to engage in some lighthearted mischievousness.

For me, sometimes this naughtiness comes in the form of kicking off my shoes and watching *Oprah* for an hour in my office in the middle of my workday. Sometimes it comes in the form of a cupcake to get me through a dreary afternoon. Sometimes it takes the form of sending funny e-mails from someone else's computer when she or he has popped to the restroom and waiting for the confused receiver to send a befuddled response. Letting your hair down is a good thing. Laughter really is the best medicine, and misbehaving makes you feel young again.

A few rules to being naughty: You should never do anything to anyone else that you wouldn't want to be done to you (a new twist on the old golden rule). It should always be legal. And you should never feel guilty. Because if you know you're going to regret being naughty, there's no fun in it.

DON'T JUST TAKE IT FROM ME . . .

"Looking back on my twenties, I had a hot poker stuck up my ass and a plum in my mouth for too long. I didn't approve of drinking; I didn't approve of random moments of physical abandon. I certainly didn't understand why someone would be so silly as to take out a loan to go on vacation. I don't know what made me mellow out, but the older I get, the more I want to try new things and find out what people are raving about. I'm not naughty yet, but I'm certainly learning to indulge the fun side of me."

Marcella, 33, production manager, Boston

"I used to think being naughty meant being sexual. But now I know it's having that extra cookie, or sneaking off for an afternoon nap, or laughing at the couple in the restaurant who can't stop kissing. Anything that makes you feel young again and like a bit of a minx is good for you."

Amanda, 28, accounts clerk, Omaha, Nebraska

IF YOU CAN'T EMBRACE YOUR NAUGHTY SIDE . . .

Try not to judge others who can. We all have different standards and values we live by. You might think someone prancing around the office or singing on the subway is daft, but who cares? Admire her or his spirit and leave judgments tucked away. We are all different, and that's what makes life interesting.

83 Dig Through Your Dad's Music Collection

I can still remember the first time I heard Dire Straits. Okay, so they aren't perhaps the greatest rock gods of all time, but they're pretty good. I was eleven years old, in the backseat of my dad's car, being driven to the local swimming pool on a Saturday, and "Brothers in Arms" came on. I was spellbound.

To my amazement and absolute delight, my dad had all their albums and encouraged me to have a listen. And while I was searching through, looking for more Dire Straits, I encountered Fleetwood Mac, the Beatles, the Bee Gees, Barbra Streisand, Barry Manilow, the Beach Boys, Elton John, and Carly Simon. Not a bad day for me musically, that.

Of course I rushed around acting as though I'd uncovered some great secret, a musical gift I could share with my friends and younger brothers. I didn't realize these artists already had worldwide acclaim, countless Grammys, and drug habits. To me they were new and fresh.

This is how dads and their record collections can provide a great musical education. Dads—by their very nature of being grown-up men with not much spare time on their hands—cut through the bullshit. You can jump on their musical bandwagon for a quick introduction to the history of great music.

So ask your dad to get out his boxes of records. It will be good for both of you—he can get nostalgic and be flattered you're admiring his taste, and you can hear something new and perhaps find a new favorite musician. Most of the time, golden oldies are called so for a reason.

DON'T JUST TAKE IT FROM ME . . .

"My dad is such a Beatles fan that I decided to become one, too, initially just because I wanted an excuse to bond with him. He is a quiet man, not prone to opening up, and music felt like an easy route to get to know him. Now I don't have to pretend, of course—I've got all the Beatles albums and three T-shirts. My

NO REGRETS

dad doesn't say much, but I know he's thrilled we share something so meaningful."

Jennifer, 31, shop manager, Las Vegas, Nevada

"I have an encyclopedic knowledge of music, and I put it down to the household I grew up in. We always had the radio on, my dad was always listening to new things enthusiastically, and my older brothers were always going off to various rock gigs. Now I love every genre of music, from every decade. My friends get stuck with hip-hop or R & B, and they don't even recognize a Marvin Gaye song when it comes on. I feel bad for them for missing out."

Cassandra, 26, student, Miami, Florida

IF YOU CAN'T DIG THROUGH YOUR DAD'S MUSIC COLLECTION . . .

Dig through his memories instead—it will help you to understand him, your mother, and your family dynamic. My favorite story about a dad opening up to his daughter is from when an acquaintance was in Nairobi. She'd been born there, but this was her first trip back since she had left as a three-year-old. Her mother had recently passed away in London and she and her father missed her terribly, so she called her father to tell him where she was: in the hospital ward where she had been born fifty years before. Her father's voice caught with emotion as he asked her, "See the window on the far right, looking out over the courtyard? See the drainpipe beneath it?" She did. "I climbed that drainpipe the night you were born to sneak some champagne in to your mother for us to have a private celebration. We were so excited to have you." Of course, my acquaintance collapsed in tears, as did her father on the phone line back in England. Dads often have a lot of wisdom and feelings to impart—you just have to find a way of getting them to open up.

84 Spend Time with Your Grandma

No one has the perfect family but there is ultimately something remarkably warm, comfortable, and reassuring about them.

I was always pretty laissez-faire about my little clan. It wasn't until I moved four thousand miles away that I realized how important our bond, our blood, and our innate support of one another actually was. I can survive being so far away from them because I know I'll go home someday, and a few years apart for me and my brothers will feel like nothing in the grand sweep of our future worlds of work, partners, new houses, and children.

But I feel differently about my grandma. Apart from my mother, she is the only woman in the world who loves me unconditionally. She knows everything about me, from being born to being a woman, and doesn't judge—well, not too harshly, anyway.

Grandmas, of course, don't tend to stick around for as long as parents or siblings. That's why you should really hang out with yours now, while you can.

What can you learn from your grandma?

She is your personal link to the history of a world

that she was part of half a century before you existed. Your town, your great-great-grandma, your surname, how your mother and father fell in love. She could be the greatest storyteller you ever encounter.

Make sure that when she dies, her stories don't die with her.

You can learn all about your DNA and your body's plans for the future—how much weight you'll gain and where, what troublesome ailments might come your way, and how your face will change and age. Remember things about her that you should avoid when you get to her age. I've promised my mother if she ever grows whiskers or hisses when she laughs like Gran, I'm to tell her. And soon I'll have my own little list, I'm sure—from Gran and from my mum!

You can also learn a lot about your mom, perhaps more than she will ever tell you herself. Through your gran's eyes, you can really gauge the impact you've had on your mother's life, how much she adores you, and how much fun you had together when you were a baby. Your grandma can also tell you—year by year—how you and your mom compare and what makes you different.

So don't groan and think of seeing the old dear as a chore or a bore. Talk to her. Ask questions about the past. And make the most of this walking embodiment of family life and your roots.

DON'T JUST TAKE IT FROM ME . . .

"My nana was a fighter. Her husband—my grandfather—deserted her with seven children and no money in the 1950s. But did she crumble? No way. She raised her family to be hardworking and decent and never said a bad word about men or marriage. She loved all her children and grandchildren so much that the day she died was the saddest of my life. But I was lucky enough to get to know her. She taught me that life teaches you a few lessons—they're not always nice ones, but you do learn and you can improve."

Juliet, 34, writer, Boston, Massachusetts

"My grandma can make me laugh like no one else. Her political incorrectness is so out of control, but somehow she gets away with it. She's offensive in the sweetest old-lady way, and her outdated opinions really allow me and my siblings to check in with what we believe and how the world has changed. She's a living link to the past and a guide to our moral future."

Maria, 26, bank assistant, Trenton,
New Jersey

IF YOU CAN'T SPEND TIME WITH YOUR GRANDMA . . .

Find another elderly woman to befriend. The later years can be lonely for many women as their friends and family pass away and their health makes it harder for them to get out and make new friends. Occasionally take a pie or fresh flowers to a neighbor, befriend a friend's grandma and visit her when no one else is around, and stay close to your mom—so hopefully your daughter can have a great relationship with her grandmother one day.

85 Keep Old Letters—and Write New Ones

I don't know about you, but very little sunshine comes out of my mailbox. I tend to get bills, fliers for things I don't need, and bank statements. So in a bid to receive more interesting, heartwarming post, my new resolution is to send more interesting, heart-warming post. E-mail is easy, texts are cheap, and phone calls are necessary, but oh, to communicate the old-fashioned way!

If you ever find yourself in London, make a point of visiting the British Museum. There is a marvelous library there, and in glass cabinets you can read the world's great letters—romantic and otherwise—handwritten by some of the most famous people who ever lived. Within the scrawl, you can feel Elizabeth I's growing panic about the safety of England and her cousin's treachery. On the page, you can sense Jane Austen's wit and wisdom outside the confines of her humorous novels. Whether communicating with friends or other world leaders, Winston Churchill proved himself to be a man of astounding character.

Letters capture a moment, a mood. The sender has sat and deliberated over words in a way that modern communication doesn't allow. And a handwritten letter is appreciated and pored over in a way that a quick read and a delete of a text could never convey.

So when someone does send you a letter, keep it somewhere safe. Appreciate the effort and the thought behind it, and find a special box or drawer that you can put it in and delve into on a rainy day or in a quiet moment of loneliness.

I often look back to the letters my little brothers wrote me when I was away at university. It's hard to imagine how my two dynamic, strapping siblings could have once mused about missing me so much—and felt the urge to draw pictures of home and my parents. The teenage letters from friends have also proved to be artifacts of great importance: did we really fancy him or care so much about that pop group? Apparently so! Now if I tried to imagine being in the head of a fifteen-year-old love-struck girl, I couldn't—but within the pages of these letters, I am once again a besotted pimply teen with a love of literature.

So brighten someone's postbox, and your days will brighten, too.

DON'T JUST TAKE IT FROM ME . . .

"Today with the Internet, the art of letter writing is lost. My grandmother would send me letters all the time. She had a lovely old-style way of writing and I'd treasure them. I've still got them all bundled up together in a plastic box in the attic. They were always the cutest cards; she would go to Hallmark and collect ones that would mean something to me. My grandmother raised me from a young age, so they mean so much now that I don't have her physically around me anymore."

Michelle, 42, yoga teacher, Greenwich, Connecticut

"I have always been a letter writer and would stay in touch with my large and geographically challenged family with cards at special times. It was a hassle to write so many as the family grew and grew, but something inside told me to keep it up. My nephew ended up marrying a real snob whom the family wasn't keen on, but my attitude toward her changed when she thanked me for sending letters to her son, my great-nephew. She said it was lovely for her boy to get something through the post and that he kept them under his bed—and it helped her to motivate him to write thank-you letters after Christmas, too!"

Jill, 55, homemaker, Kansas City, Missouri

IF YOU CAN'T KEEP OLD LETTERS AND WRITE NEW ONES . . .

Flip through your book collection and put any with nice inscriptions in them to one side. You don't want them ending up in a charity shop in a moment of spring-cleaning fever, and the inscriptions will forever remind you of the person who wrote the note. And if you can't write new letters, why not? Take five minutes each Sunday to write to someone new. Trust me—it'll be worth it for the recipient.

86 Take Up a Hobby—Just for You, Just for Fun

When you're feeling frustrated and/or bored with areas of your life—especially those you can't change—hobbies are a great thing to take on. Go to your community college and check out the courses offered. The world is full of new, wonderful, kooky, surprising pastimes that you can make your own. Pursuing something for yourself is a great tool for getting to know who you really are and where your secret talents lie.

As a child, hobbies are thrust upon you by pushy parents, demanding schools, or college entrance papers. As an adult, hobbies offer some "me time," the simplest form of escapism from a hectic job or unhappy home. And you never know what useful skills you will pick up along the way that could be transplanted into your career or relationships. I have always loved photography but never really knew what to do with my fondness until I stumbled across a brochure on courses at the local adult-education center. Without thinking, I signed up for two years of photography. For three evenings per week, I would have to attend lectures and seminars, and at the end of each year, I would need to produce course work and take exams—but far from putting me off, I devoured the idea. For once, I was choosing to take an exam and be judged. No one else was telling me to.

It was the perfect escape. In my class, where no one knew me, I was free to just be me and not someone's wife, employee, or daughter.

DON'T JUST TAKE IT FROM ME . . .

"Upon returning to work after maternity leave, I felt confused and unable to keep my worlds straight. Back in the workplace I had to concentrate on business and keeping my boss happy, and then at home it was all about the baby. My mother could see

NO REGRETS

how unhappy I was and suggested my husband and I—who was feeling mightily left out and stressed out, too—take a night out once a week together and she'd babysit. My mother is a genius—we joined a salsa class and adore it. We feel fit and always laugh, and it's such a sexy dance that it's even improved our sex life."

Denise, 36, researcher, San Antonio, Texas

"I started doing yoga because my then husband's cooking was making me fat and my knees were starting to hurt. The very handsome man that I practiced with helped me stay on my mat when I was tired and wanted to give up. Standing on one leg next to a man who looked like a hot Jesus wasn't the reason I left my husband—I was leaving him anyway—but the confidence I got from yoga and the hot Jesus was the final push. So the hobby meant a lot to me."

Noelle, 29, makeup artist, Boulder, Colorado

IF YOU CAN'T TAKE UP A HOBBY . . .

Somehow make some time for yourself for pure enjoyment. If your commute is long and tedious, download your favorite television or radio shows onto an iPod and the dreary minutes will be transformed. If you can't leave the house, think about new things you can try at home—even if it's just making notes during cooking shows or learning about new countries on the Travel Channel. It will make you a happier, calmer person.

CHIC GEEK

87 Rediscover "Take on Me"

I'm a happy person on the whole, but if one song could capture all my happiest moments and mix them into the most delicious Cold Stone Creamery concoction ever, it would be A-ha's "Take on Me."

It hit the top spot on the Billboard charts in the mid-eighties. Many people think the success was due to the comic-strip video and sexy band members, but I think it was the brilliance of the pumping piano and hook. Indeed, as the video and band members have been ravaged by time, the song stands strong.

That tune has got me out of a wealth of inertia, immobility, and grumpiness. There's something about the high-pitched chorus that makes it impossible not to sing along to. Loudly!

It's become somewhat of an anthem of good times for me. It's the one song my two younger brothers and I truly agree on. Every New Year's Eve at my parents' shindig, we play it right after the more traditional "Auld Lang Syne" (it's what you need after that sweet but dreary number) and everyone perks up. Our pièce de résistance is an Ivens group air-keyboard performance in the middle of the song.

It always seems to be playing when good things are happening. Because people who know me associate me with it, I get texts from all over the world exclaiming, "I'm at a beach bar in Italy/eighties disco in London/family wedding in San Diego and they're playing A-ha!" They're having a fab time, and I'm flattered they're thinking of me.

Give it a play. If you're having a good time, it will make it even better when the beats start hitting and the people around you start to recall why they loved the song all those years ago.

If you're having a bad time—even if you're just a bit tired and it's raining outside—press play and watch the clouds disperse. Just watch out for valuable objects and people's faces—you will want to jump up and down and flail your arms around!

DON'T JUST TAKE IT FROM ME . . .

"I was in love with Morten Harket, the lead singer of A-ha—I think it was the gap in his teeth and the way he wore a denim jacket. To be honest, the whole band was quite sexy. I was totally disappointed they turned out to be one-hit wonders and I couldn't justify having their poster up on my bedroom wall for very long."

Kristen, 32, banker, New York City

"It's all very well being cool and liking the latest tunes, but sometimes you've just got to embrace your bad, sad taste in music and have fun. "Take on Me" is one of those songs that you can't sit down to. And it amazes me the number of times I play it in my car and people screech, 'I love this song—what is it? I haven't heard it for years!'"

Hayley, 33, homemaker, London

Revisit the English bands of the eighties. The foot-stomping, joy-promoting classic "Come on Eileen" by Dexys Midnight Runners cannot fail to raise a smile. If you have a rational phobia (although I disagree—what's not to love about blue eyeliner and Rubik's Cubes?) of all things eighties, shift forward a few decades. You cannot remain miserable or unmoved by the amazing talent of Mika on his album *Love Today.* Be open to music and the positive effect it can have on your life—be it fifty years old or being played for the first time on VH1 tonight.

88 Indulge in a Great Work of Literature

There is nothing more divine than curling up with a fabulous book on a wet and cold afternoon. Cozied up in flannel pajamas, bolstered by hot tea and cookies, I love how every fresh page brings moments of pure in-dulgence.

The art of enjoying good books—or loafing around with literature, as I prefer to call it—is a lost one these days.

I'm a magazine editor and a newspaper writer so I shouldn't be saying this, but *slow down*—read some-thing that has a shelf life longer than a pint of milk. The Internet has pushed us even further away from our childhood days of flashlights under duvets, trying to squeeze in a few more chapters of Nancy Drew before our moms tell us to get some sleep. We're in such a rush, we want more information now, and we want details and story lines to hit us in the face.

I was out for a cocktail with some friends recently, and one of them launched in on a story about her book club and the fun they have, sipping gin and tonics and discussing Ian McEwan. "We loved *Saturday,* so we're determined to read *Atonement* by summer, but we've got to enjoy *The Namesake* first," she rambled on, excited about her literary ambitions. I looked down at my Birkenstocks. I was ashamed. I hadn't read a book in more than a month. And worse still, I hadn't got swept away by a moving, sincere novel in more than a year. I'd been filling what little spare time I did have with chick lit, the biographies of media darlings, and cookbooks. These all have their places of course, but they're not great conversation pieces and probably won't stand the test of time.

I decided to embark on a journey of historically relevant and fabulously entertaining works by great New York authors—everyone from Edith Wharton to Jay McInerney. Barnes & Noble felt the strength of my credit card that miserable afternoon, when my hands grabbed beautifully crisp tomes from the shelves and my legs walked toward the checkout. But I haven't regretted it. I've never thought, *What a waste of a weekend!*

We're all busy, and sometimes bookshops or Amazon.com can be daunting. But if you've got the time and inclination to enjoy some books that will make you see the world a little differently, try these, my top five: *Rebecca* by Daphne du Maurier, *Wuthering*

Heights by Emily Brontë, *The Age of Innocence* by Edith Wharton, *Pride and Prejudice* by Jane Austen, and *Valley of the Dolls* by Jacqueline Susann (perhaps not such a classic in the vein of the others, but a great story nonetheless).

In these great works, women come alive and make you feel normal, excited, encouraged, and emotional—you'll want to read the books more than once. That's the great thing about great works of literature: the characters remain your friends, allies, and heroines long after you've turned the last page.

DON'T JUST TAKE IT FROM ME . . .

"My voracious love of reading began at age four when I was given *Chocolate Mouse and Sugar Pig*, a story about how two confectionary animals stage their getaway from a shop to avoid being eaten. It taught me that the imagination is a far more extraordinary medium than any TV show or movie could ever be. Since then I have accrued a mile-long list of books I love. If you have the stomach for Middle English, *Sir Gawain and the Green Knight* is the only truly perfect text I have ever read; the naughty bits of Chaucer are always worth a giggle; Jane Austen is unbeatable for the machinations of love. For a light brain tickle, you can't go wrong with Carl Hiaasen, Jasper Fforde, and Jilly Cooper."
Ruth, 29, journalist, Los Angeles

"My love of books has allowed the dullest moments of my life to pass in a whirl of seventeenth-century swashbuckling, eighteenth-century decadence, and nineteenth-century romance. Whether I'm commuting or stuck on a queue, a fine book lifts me from the doldrums and places me into a new, exciting adventure. My father fell ill last summer, and my family and I kept vigil for weeks on end. Reading my father's favorite works allowed me to honor him."

Vanessa, 38, florist, San Francisco, California

IF YOU CAN'T INDULGE IN A GREAT WORK OF LITERATURE . . .

Well, firstly, of course you can, so stop making excuses and read. But more diplomatically, if some of the old English tomes scare you, start on other modern classics that every woman adores—*Lace* by Shirley Conran and *The Thorn Birds* by Colleen McCullough are sweeping histories of tragic deaths and enraging passions. And if you still can't force yourself to pick up a book, go audio. Download talking books and listen to them while you're at the gym or doing housework. It's not quite the same, but at least you won't be mistaken for an ignoramus at your next dinner party.

89 Make a Family Tree

Who do you think you are? That's not just a random question posed by those girl-power advocates of the 1990s, the Spice Girls. It's a serious dilemma. We all need to know where we come from, the stories that have shaped our past, and the quirks original to our family alone.

I'm not going to get all morbid on your ass, but before people start dropping off, dying off, and disappearing, it would be of great value to you and future generations if you gathered up info and stored it for all your family to share.

History is a joy anyway, but your personal history—what could be better?

I made a family tree when I was a teenager, researching names and dates at my local church and library and pumping my family for information. I remember sitting earnestly with bits of paper, different-colored felt-tips and sticky tape, and a list of strange people who shared my name. Some were French, I was dismayed to discover (it's an English thing), and a few were war heroes. The family tree gave me a sense of roots and pride that is all too difficult to grasp in this fast-paced, quick-consumption world we live in.

So interview your parents, your grandparents, aunts, uncles, and cousins. Dig around in the attic for old legal papers and photos. Delving into your family's past and making a family tree won't tell you everything about who you are, but it will help to place your family as a collective in history for generations to come.

DON'T JUST TAKE IT FROM ME . . .

"A cousin I'd long since forgotten about contacted me through a Web site called Genes Reunited a few years ago. At first I thought, *I have enough trouble keeping up with my immediate family; I don't need more hangers-on.* But my dismissive attitude was wrong. She sent me a few photos, and I could see the family resemblance (we're not blessed with the smallest noses)—it made me laugh. We haven't met up yet, but I've sent her all the info I know so she can put together a family tree that I know I will treasure."

Joyce, 42, homemaker, London

"I traveled back to the village my parents came from in Ireland last year. Through a research company, I had discovered the names and birth dates of my predecessors, and I was able to visit the churches I knew ancestors had got married in. It was a deeply spiritual experience. I felt at home."

Claire, 35, stylist, Brooklyn, New York

IF YOU CAN'T MAKE A FAMILY TREE . . .

Explore someone else's family history and take a trip to Ellis Island in New York City. It's a deeply moving experience and a fabulous day out. After all, it's where America as we know it began and established New York as the cultural melting pot of the world.

BEAUTY MAVEN

90 Get a Smile You'll Be Proud to Flash

A few months ago I did the most controversial thing I have ever done: I got veneers. This doesn't sound like a hot topic, but by golly, it inspired a lot of discussion and criticism. I'd never liked my smile—partly because I've got a mouth so small that I can barely shove in my Häagen-Dazs dulce de leche without getting it down my chin, and partly because I have—or had, I should say—the teeth of a shark. No one else saw that far back in my mouth, but it still made me self-conscious.

British people are famous for having terrible teeth. We're not a vain race, so dental perfection falls somewhere near the bottom of a list of beauty projects, along with electrolysis and a high-protein diet. My teeth weren't at an Austin Powers level of hideousness, but I'd never gotten them whitened or straightened. So I hit age thirty-two with these strange predator-style fangs in a little rosebud mouth. Odd.

During a drunken night out, a fellow Brit friend of mine confessed that he'd got veneers a few years after moving to the States. He suggested I go to his dentist, because when he first met me, he "didn't see the blond hair or big boobs or think, *Ooh, she's tall!*" He thought, *That girl's got to be British—she's got teeth like Count Dracula!*

I got the phone number for his dentist and made an appointment for the following week. Having an awkward smile had damaged my confidence, and I wanted teeth to be proud of. And dental health is something that is often neglected, and I wanted to make sure I had healthy teeth and gums, too. Now was the time.

Everyone from the receptionist to the dentist had dazzling—fake—smiles. I was sold. It was expensive, and for a few weeks after getting my veneers fitted, it felt as if I had a live wire of electricity running through my gums, but it was worth every dollar.

Word quickly spread of what I'd done. Well, I couldn't really hide it, could I? And I didn't want to! My first visit home to England after the work was a trying time. Friends were texting and calling, saying they'd heard a rumor I had new teeth. You see, this seems such a shallow thing to do in the UK.

But the first time someone told me I had perfect teeth, I knew I'd done the right thing.

We should feel happy about ourselves. And I'm all about self-improvement. Yes, I could have lived with my teeth, but I had the money to change them and I found a great person to help me.

Invest in yourself. Invest in your teeth. Healthy gums and strong teeth are one of the best investments you can make for your future. I'm not just talking about getting something as drastic as veneers—having your teeth whitened or wearing braces can make all the difference.

Having teeth of which I feel proud has inspired me to do more than the twice-a-day quick brush. Dentist Debra taught me to floss properly (yes, go up into the gums, and hug the side of each tooth, going up and down for a few seconds), get regular checkups, and visit the hygienist.

The old saying goes that a smile costs nothing. Mine sure wasn't free, but that's okay, because it's a confident smile now.

DON'T JUST TAKE IT FROM ME . . .

"After years of feeling like Bugs Bunny, I got my teeth straightened and filed down to an acceptable nonrabbit size. It has turned my life around. I can smile now and mean it!"

Jill, 40, teacher, Billings, Montana

"It hurt like hell and cost me a small fortune, but the sleepless nights and bank loan were worth it. I went to a cosmetic surgeon and asked for teeth like Julia Roberts, and my dream came true. Don't jump into any cosmetic surgery or dentistry lightly, but do tweak here and there if it will make you happy."

Ebony, 35, food manager, Wichita, Kansas

IF YOU CAN'T GET A SMILE YOU'LL BE PROUD TO FLASH . . .

At least make sure you're doing the basics—gum disease can lead to heart disease. Brush at least twice a day, floss, don't overindulge in sugary sweets, get regular checkups, and use good toothpaste.

91 Get Mani-Pedis with Your Mates

There's something so ridiculously girlie about getting your nails done that I think we should celebrate it. I live in New York, where nail bars lure you on every corner with fluorescent signs offering a manicure and pedicure for ridiculously low prices. When my English friends fly over the pond to see me, it's the first stop we make on our tour round Manhattan. Forget the Empire State Building or Ellis Island; my friends associate these spa shops as the most marvelous thing America has given the modern world.

Bonding with your friends and getting beautiful is a genius way of multitasking. Doing two of your favorite things at the same time can only double the pleasure.

My mother's generation wasn't as lucky as mine. At thirty-two, my mum was busy raising two young kids and working hard to feed the family. Now here I am: no kids; a good, hard-earned salary; and spare time to pamper myself—with the other thirty-something, childless, free friends of mine. I really enjoy this aspect of my life. And I've introduced my mum to it in the most decadent style. When she comes over to see me, I take her to a beauty salon with prices that limit it to very special occasions, and we sit in massage chairs for a good few hours. We sip champagne and nibble on cookies and berries while we get bathed, exfoliated, massaged, and decorated. We have a lovely afternoon. It's just for the girls. Yes, men have their purposes, but some things are better when it's just the ladies. Getting a mani-pedi is definitely one of those things.

DON'T JUST TAKE IT FROM ME . . .

"I've got a series of photos that always makes me smile. They are photos of my feet, with brightly colored, painted nails and buffed heels, lying on a variety of sun loungers on beaches around the world. Take a photo of your feet and you'll always remember that feeling of sun and sand and what you looked at in those beautiful places."

Laura, 26, sales assistant, London

"My friends and I are all in our twenties and struggling with our careers and making names for ourselves. Having time out during the week is impossible, so we meet for manicures on Saturday mornings to unwind and analyze our week in one go. I love my Saturdays."

Suzy, 28, hedge-fund manager, New York City

IF YOU CAN'T GET MANI-PEDIS WITH YOUR MATES . . .

If you're having a tight month, stay in and hold a spa night chez vous. Tell your friends to bring a couple bottles (of wine and nail polish) and decorate one another's fingers and toes. You won't do such a nice job—especially after the copious bottles of wine—but it's bonding and will make you look prettier than doing nothing at all.

92 Go (Completely) Bare Down There

It's all very well getting your "lady garden" mowed and trimmed, but please, I urge you to do so carefully. I have a horror story. A horror story so ghastly that it still gives me a nightmare every time I have to prepare for a beach holiday and contemplate sorting out my nether regions. We don't want to walk around with furry armpits or chimplike legs, and goddammit, a sleek bikini line is a thing of great beauty, but heed my tale.

I'd been a regular wax-on, wax-off kinda gal for a few years when I decided (spurred on by enthusiastic, hair-free pals) to get a Brazilian wax. For those of you who don't know, this means a clean sweep down below. The whole lot is ripped off. This idea had never appealed to me before, but I fancied a summer of skimpy bikinis and I fell to my usual position that you should try most things once in your life. I decided to go to my local waxing salon and request they leave just a little strip.

What can I say? The sweet Russian lady who whisked me downstairs into her workshop seemed to know what she was doing. I wasn't mildly embarrassed whipping off my drawers and, knees akimbo, displaying my wares. And she was efficient. With six dollops of wax and at least four yelps of pain, I was as smooth as a peach (except for the aforementioned strip) and very happy. I tipped her generously—you have to after that task, right?—and left.

A few weeks later my bikini line declared war on me.

Other waxers had told me that my hair grew in different directions and had taken their time when doing a standard wax, and I thought it a little strange that my Russian lady had performed a Brazilian in half the time. Yes, it turned out to be very odd. Uh-huh. Because there had been no regard for hair patterns, stubble was now starting to emerge in a form of worrying lumps, bumps, and awful spots. I was horrified. This wasn't the sleek summer look I had planned. I went to another beautician, who gasped when I flashed her a look. "Who did this to you?" she asked in horror. "A nice lady who wanted to take her lunch break, I think," I replied, looking away from the battleground below. She did the best she could to repair the damage, and for the next few months we battled on with the ingrown hairs.

So do wax, but don't go cheap and cheerful. Talk to your friends and ask for recommendations. As soon as I alerted a few of my friends to my issues, they offered phone numbers of many a waxing wonder woman, and those waxers are now on speed dial. Do the same.

DON'T JUST TAKE IT FROM ME . . .

"I was once pulled and pinched and waxed so much, I was left with a private area resembling a nasty plucked turkey before it's cooked. Don't go for the notion that it's all or nothing. Sometimes a little goes a long way!"

Jessica, 31, hotel receptionist, Sonoma, California

"Going bare is all I ever do. I feel so fresh and clean, like a new woman. I feel groomed and confident. You feel free almost. I love it."

Loraine, 35, stylist, Queens

IF YOU CAN'T GO (COMPLETELY) BARE DOWN THERE . . .

Find another sufficient depilatory service. If you don't fancy sharing your bits and pieces with a stranger, do it yourself. A friend with sensitive skin uses a hair-removal cream with great success. Another friend shaves and coats her bits with Tend Skin (a miracle lotion) to stop the associated rash. If you're feeling really rich, determined, and up for a bit of pain, get the whole lot off with a series of laser treatments.

93 Wear Sunscreen

I spent many vacations with the girls, all of us shining in the sun, coated in baby oil. We'd venture into the swimming pool to cool down and leave an oil slick behind us.

Now, ten years after learning a few difficult lessons, I've finally got my SPF, my sun protection factor—the higher the better. I've learned—and you should, too—that even going as high as SPF 50 will allow you to get a slight glow, a golden color instead of burned bits and leathery skin.

I left it a little late to learn how to take care in the sun and I regret that. But it's better late than never. I apply and reapply at least SPF 25 (UVA/UVB) lotion, avoid the midday sun, and know when enough is enough.

However pretty you look with a tan, you're gonna look prettier with fewer wrinkles and all the other skin damage that too much sun brings. Oh, and you'll look prettier alive, too. Skin cancer is the most common form of cancer in the United States, and the best prevention is being careful in the sun.

So, as the aptly named "Everybody's Free (to Wear Sunscreen)" song goes, "If I could offer you only one tip for the future, sunscreen would be it."

DON'T JUST TAKE IT FROM ME . . .

"When I was in college, I asked one of my favorite teachers how old he was and he said thirty-five. I was amazed that he had not one wrinkle on his face. He told me that he always wore sunscreen. Back in 1986, no one wore sunscreen on a daily basis. I decided that I was going to follow his lead. I've been wearing it religiously ever since. I think at almost forty-four, I look pretty damn good!"

Olga, 43, designer, New York City

"Remember the next-door neighbor in *There's Something About Mary*? She exists. Every time I hit a vacation hot spot, I see women with dried-out, old boobies and faces that suggest they were raised by a family of raisins. And they're only forty years old. That's enough to get me smothering myself with sunblock."

Janice, 29, restaurant manager, San Diego

IF YOU CAN'T WEAR SUNSCREEN . . .

You better get your ass to a pharmacy and stock up on some antiaging moisturizer. I'm being flippant, of course. There is no reason not to wear sunscreen and wear it well. You will still get a tan, but you might not get cancer.

94 Shape Your Brows

The perfect arch takes work but not much. Don't waste any more time living as a unibrowed freak or caterpillar-harboring monster. Take a good, hard look at your face and get to work. A *Blue Lagoon* Brooke Shields brow works only on Brooke Shields.

Grab a pencil and go to a mirror in good light. Hold the pencil against the left side of your nose and pluck anything above the nose to the right of the pencil. Now place the pencil against the right side, and pluck those stray hairs to the left. This should give you two clearly defined brows.

Now pluck underneath each brow, following the curve and snipping out any stray hairs—even the fair ones. Never pluck above the natural line of a brow. If you find it hard to work out the right shape, invest in a brow stencil (found at any beauty store). The stencil fixes onto your brow, you pluck around it, and—voilà!—a fabulous brow shape. A new, improved you!

While you're there with the tweezers, have a quick check round the rest of your face for spare hairs. Going out on a date with a stray chin whisker is totally regrettable.

Check in with your brows once a week when you're doing a big groom. I do mine on Sunday nights. It's a peaceful way to start the week: deep conditioning my hair, applying a face mask, shaving my legs, shaping my brows . . . I start the week in shipshape and Bristol fashion, as we Cockneys say.

If the hair is a bit sparse, pencil in your brows or even consider getting them dyed (I do this when I'm going on vacation so I can look semidecent without any makeup on). Never go more than two shades darker than your hair color, whatever that color is at the time. Too dark and you'll shape your brows, all right, but you'll also add ten years to your age.

DON'T JUST TAKE IT FROM ME . . .

"Beautifully shaped eyebrows can lift your eyes, enhance your cheekbones, and make you look groomed. They can slim your face and make you look younger. Pluck, yeah!"

Katie, 29, beauty therapist, Nashville

"I overplucked as a teenager, and it's taken years for me to get my brows looking healthy again. Now I really appreciate the difference a good grooming can make to your face. Now that I no longer have to draw on nonexistent brows, friends say I look younger and softer. I love it!"

Kristen, 25, financial planner, Boston

BEAUTY MAVEN

Go into a department store—they'll do it there as part of a customized makeover, often for free. Just make sure they don't overpluck to make you look like them. Be firm. Keep an eye on their tweezer action. Brows never grow back the same.

95 Find the Perfect Red Lipstick for You

The definition of glamour? A red pout. Unquestionably sexy and confident, a drag of red across the lips screams style. A smudged crimson smile can even suggest naughty. Every woman must have her pocket rocket of glamour—she just needs to find the right shade to flatter her skin tone.

If you have fair skin, you could be in trouble, so try as many shades as possible—on your lips and on the back of your hand—to get the perfect one. You don't want to overwhelm the eyes with a big red kisser, but you do want to look immaculate. And make your skin as flawless as possible. Ask for help at a beauty counter in your favorite store, or experiment with a few shades and ask an honest pal for her opinion.

Other rules to learn and follow for the perfect red pout? Don't forget primer—there is nothing worse than smudged red lips or lipstick on your teeth. Prime up to keep your lipstick in place from cocktail hour to the end of the night. Follow primer with a lip liner, and then use a brush to apply the lipstick with precision. Don't rush (it's not a clear gloss and mistakes can be seen a mile off!), and use a mirror—but not a car mirror in a moving vehicle, madam. And don't be inspired by a red dress to wear red lipstick. That's too matchy matchy. Red lips look best when you're wearing dark, somber colors.

DON'T JUST TAKE IT FROM ME . . .

"Anytime a woman wants to feel pretty or done up, she wears red lips. She'll get the attention of the entire room when she walks in. But it's not just for men—the woman does it for herself. It makes her feel glamorous. It's not an old look; it's a sophisticated look."

Colleen, 24, beauty editor, Cleveland

"My husband fell in love with me the day he saw me wear red lipstick. Well, that's what he says, anyway. It was our third date, and I thought it was because we had started to feel comfortable with each other, had had a real laugh, and had fallen into bed. But no. He says it's because I was irresistible to him with my scarlet pout!"

Jane, 32, accountant, Memphis

IF YOU CAN'T FIND THE PERFECT RED LIPSTICK . . .

Give up—we can't all be perfect at everything. Go to a makeup counter and ask for tips on what color and texture would suit your mouth, your skin, and your teeth. Some mauve shades can turn teeth yellow!

96 Get Contact Lenses

My eyesight started to deteriorate the minute I left university and started working, sitting in front of a computer all day long. I didn't notice for a while because my working life started at the same time as my booze-fueled nights out in London. Catching the Tube home late at night, I'd struggle to read the signs unless I was standing next to them, but I assumed that it was the fault of my wine-induced double vision. This tipsy midnight squinting continued until I realized I couldn't see the television on quiet nights at home.

For the next ten years I battled with a variety of glasses, which I would invariably lose, sit on, forget, or scuff up in the bottom of my handbag.

If I went on vacation, I'd have to choose between seeing the sights or protecting my eyes from the sun (I refused to wear prescription sunglasses because they were so ugly). Skiing was hell—I'd steam up the minute I got to the top of a mountain and have to practically use my intuition to get down the slope in one piece (I often misread directions and would head down scary blue runs instead of green, which, to be honest, may have sped up my learning!).

Eventually, enough was enough and I did what my grown-up friends had done years before: I got contact lenses.

The optometrist was underwhelmed by my bravery. I expected an encouraging smile and a warm welcome, a lollipop and a gold star. I got a gruff request for my health-insurance details and was told to sit on a stool in front of the eye contraption. There were no bells and whistles, just a quick test and a lesson in how to get the lenses in and out without impaling my eyeballs (it's much easier than a lens virgin would ever imagine). Leaving the store was a revelation. I could see! Through the rain I could see colors, faces, and billboards, all without the threat of steam. Why oh why hadn't I embraced these little petals of plastic before? I'd been scared and lazy, without reason. Lenses really are easy to use and look after—and once I put them in for the day, I'm worry free.

DON'T JUST TAKE IT FROM ME . . .

"As a beauty tip, removing glasses from the equation really helps accessorizing. Glasses can bulk up the face and distract the eye from good makeup or pretty jewelry. Lenses allowed me to play around more and to feel more feminine."

Julie, 33, teacher, Oklahoma City

"You have to be careful not to get too drunk and forget to take them out, but apart from that, lenses are liberating and easy to use. I used to have to squint at signs and televisions and now I don't have to—and I'm excited that this will limit my wrinkles, too!"

Danielle, 36, bank teller, Los Angeles

BEAUTY MAVEN

Make sure you are wearing glasses that suit your face shape. I have a square-shaped face and for years did exactly the wrong thing by wearing square-shaped frames. This turned me into Little Miss SpongeBob SquareFace. Big mistake. Try on dozens of shapes and sizes and take trusted, honest friends with you to the optician's when you're splurging on a new pair of glasses.

97 Quit Smoking

Do I really need to spell out why you should do this? If the serious health issues aren't enough to make you put down those cancer sticks forever, what about this: your skin is going to age dramatically and your mouth is going to pucker up to look like a cat's asshole much quicker than the skin and mouths of your nonsmoking buddies; your taste buds are going to shrivel up and die and you won't be able to truly enjoy every morsel of chocolate soufflé anymore; you're going to get out of breath easier during sex; your dry-cleaning tab is going to soar through the roof as you try to eradicate those foul odors from your clothes; it will damage your fertility; and if a woman who smokes twenty cigarettes a day gives up the habit, she'll be able to buy a pair of Christian Louboutin shoes after about six months of saving.

Searching for an ashtray in which to stump out your last cigarette yet?

As a teenager, I spent my summers on exchange programs with a French family. I had my first cigarette at age fourteen listening to Vanessa Paradis with a precociously glamorous Gallic girl. We smoked Philip Morris Blue and drank black coffee. I felt sophisticated and incredibly grown-up. The French smoke so well, you see, in their scarcely lit, aromatic cafés by the Seine. Bicycles are lined up outside, poodles are tied to the railings, and berets are resting at jaunty angles on dark heads as the French converse about Jean-Paul Sartre through swirls of gray smoke.

Right—this all sounds fabulous, and if I were living in a 1950s Brigitte Bardot movie, it could perhaps be doable. But I'm not and neither are you and we have to be sensible.

Quitting will be one of the hardest things you'll ever have to do. My dad watched his own father have both his legs amputated due to smoking-related diseases and still my dad continued to smoke. It wasn't until he had a heart attack and the doctor told him to give it up or die that he quit. By then he'd had a triple valve transplant and a miserable year, scaring the life out of my mother. Don't wait for that to happen to you.

Go to your doctor and get advice on how to give it up. Join support groups. Even try hypnotherapy—this has worked for many of my friends. Investigate patches, injections, and chewing gum. Anything is better than continuing to light up.

Look after yourself during this testing time of withdrawal. For every day you go without a cigarette, gift yourself something (an ice cream, a magazine, an early night, a soak in the bath). Call on your nearest and dearest to support you. At trying times, when you would have reached for the deathly packet, ask your partner to de-stress you with a foot rub instead.

And sleep soundly knowing that you are overcoming the greatest health challenge you will ever face.

DON'T JUST TAKE IT FROM ME . . .

"It wasn't hard to give up. I came down with a terrible cough for ten days, and that made it easier. My skin is so much better and now I can taste stuff again. All the boys I dated and still date tend to be bad boys who smoke, but I've stayed strong and they like me for it. My lung capacity is much better and so is my breathing, which is very important for my job."

Amme, 34, yoga instructor, Tulum, Mexico

"My father worked in the tobacco industry, before we knew so much about it, and he is now very sad that he made his money this way, especially because his mother died from emphysema. I had always suffered with bronchial sickness, so about two years ago I decided to quit. It was very hard—especially during stressful times at work—but when I felt the urge, I'd visualize my lungs going black and shutting down. If I think about smoking now, I feel sick. I will never pick up a cigarette again."

Grace, 39, freelance writer, Omaha, Nebraska

IF YOU CAN'T QUIT SMOKING . . .

You're stupid. And don't you dare throw that "but I'll put on weight" argument at me. Here are your options: a tiny arse prematurely resting in a coffin, or a slightly bigger arse enjoying life. You choose. Oh, and by the way, while men might not mind women who smoke in porn films, in real life 92 percent of them would not want a smoker to be the mother of their children. Put that in your pipe and smoke it!

98 Return Your Hair to Its Childhood Color

One of the most famous hairdressers in the world once said to me, "Darling, remember what your hair color was when you were but a slip of a girl at ten years old and stick to that!" He wisely counseled me to choose a shade that allowed my skin to glow with youthful allure—but nothing too shocking—and allowed me to fantasize that I was still only twenty-one years old.

This is a good rule to remember. At ten, I was a natural blonde. Now at thirty-two, I'm an unnatural blonde who has to add highlights to bring back the golden haze of yesteryear. But it suits me. It suits my skin tone, my eye color, and—does this sound daft?—my idea of who I am.

Mousy is not me, and gray certainly doesn't fit into my game plan. So every three months I happily pay to be lightened, bleached, covered, and perfected. Now three shades lighter than my current natural dishwater blond, my hair is returned to its former childhood glory.

We've all had friends who've gone a bit mental and experimented with blue streaks or a pink Frenchy-from-*Grease* 'do. But did you ever think they looked good? You might have thought they were brave, or outrageous, or cool (in an Ally Sheedy–*The Breakfast Club* kind of way), but good? Never!

We're all tempted to be new people at times—to spice it up and try something that will make us feel different. This is where wigs and hair extensions come in. The latest ones look real and are not too expensive.

A drastic dye job, in contrast, not only damages the hair, it also takes ages to grow out. Think of all the vacation snaps and family portraits you'll ruin while you're waiting for your hair trauma to end.

I went a bit crazy once with some hair dye. I was eighteen years old and suffering from heatstroke when a friend handed me peroxide in a spray bottle. It seemed so easy. I could have hair the color of Madonna's in the "True Blue" video, rather than my natural sun-kissed variety. A few sprays and three hours of sun later, my hair was so blond that it was almost green . . . and it went from being smooth and strong into a tangled mess that felt as if it could snap and drop off at any minute. The hair was bad, and the roots were worse. I still regret that day.

But with my hair now as golden and shiny as it was back in the day, I feel brighter, prettier, and more alluring. Whether you're a blonde, brunette, or redhead, nature gave you the perfect color when you were barely old enough to appreciate it. While you still have the time to sit in a colorist's chair (and then go under the heat lamp and then get rinsed out and then go back under the heat lamp, and so on), get thee to the salon and watch your hair—and your attitude—be restored to its youthful exuberance.

DON'T JUST TAKE IT FROM ME . . .

"I'm a redhead. As a child I was called a carrottop and mocked for my pale skin and freckles, but just as I was growing into my looks and realizing that not everyone has to be a tanned blonde to be beautiful, my hair started to fade. It went from red to a kind of auburn brown. The shine faded to a flat matte. Well, I wasn't having any of it. I found a vegetable dye that reinstated my flaming dazzle, and I love it."

Claire, 33, banker, London

"My blond hair followed the typical trajectory of turning dirty blond in my teens and then light brown by the time I graduated from college. In my early and mid-twenties, I spent a ton of money on beautiful blond highlights, and my hair looked just as golden and glorious as it did when I was in first grade. When I was in my late twenties, however, I was living abroad and decided it was too much hassle to track down an expert colorist— I figured I could get used to my light brown hair and maybe even grow to like it. Wrong! I lasted a year before getting my highlights redone, and what a mousy year it was."

Michelle, 32, pharmacist, Philadelphia

IF YOU CAN'T (OKAY, DON'T WANT TO) RETURN YOUR HAIR TO ITS CHILDHOOD COLOR . . .

If you're going to choose another color, remember to make a drastic change *only in the comfort of a trusted salon.* If you're not sticking with the color nature gave you as a kid, never, ever grab some supermarket dye and fling it onto your head in the bathroom. The first time you try something radical, you need someone with a good eye who will tell you the truth. Don't just decide to dye your hair jet black—think about how this will work with your complexion and your wardrobe!

99 Learn to Get a Good Night's Sleep

There is nothing—and I mean nothing—more blissful than falling into the golden realm of slumber. I love that feeling when my body is physically and mentally united in the wish for sweet dreams and my head floats away a few minutes after it touches the pillow.

Good sleep isn't easy, though. As a child, you resented being sent up the apples and pears (stairs, in Cockney English) for fear of missing exciting adult conversation and racy snippets of television. So you fought hard not to fall asleep. As a teen, you'd have rather partied all night. And slept all day. We finally realize the value of serious shut-eye as we reach adulthood—and that's when it can elude us.

I'm a grumpy little madam without my full eight hours a night, so I've got a winning formula to secure a good night's rest.

> Don't drink caffeine after two o'clock in
>   the afternoon.
> Don't exercise (except for yoga) after
>   eight o'clock at night.
> Make your bedroom a soft nonwork

environment—that means no
television and no computer. Invest in
expensive bedding (it's worth
splurging on this, as well as on a good
mattress).

Put a soft lamp right next to the bed
that can be switched off without
disturbing anything but your arm.

Keep the bedroom between seventy-two
and seventy-four degrees; this is the
ultimate sleeping temperature.

And if you feel jittery or stressed in
the evening, take the time before
you hit the hay to have a warm
bath with lavender oil and to drink
chamomile tea.

This prebed regimen has made going to the land of dreams a delight for me. When I get new pajamas and cashmere socks at Christmas (they are always on my list for Santa), it gets even better. Bliss!

Zzzzzzzzzzz.... Your skin and soul will thank you for it.

DON'T JUST TAKE IT FROM ME . . .

"Good rest isn't just about looking better—it is absolutely necessary in order to have a good memory, to repair the body's damaged cells, and for concentration. And missing out on good, quality shut-eye increases the risk of developing diabetes, obesity, and infections. What better excuse to jump under the duvet?"

Sandra, 32, retail assistant, Columbus, Ohio

BEAUTY MAVEN

"I used to feel guilty about the total need I have to hibernate during the winter. Friends ask me out and I say no, I stop getting up early to go to the gym, and I become a recluse for a few months. But it's just my body's way of saying slow down. Now I know how important it is to rest—just as important as exercising. I've stopped feeling guilty, and I embrace my doziness."

Jessica, 29, advertising executive, Los Angeles

IF YOU CAN'T LEARN TO GET A GOOD NIGHT'S SLEEP . . .

There's probably a bigger issue you've got to deal with. Fears come out at nighttime, and worries and stress can keep you awake. What are the big issues in your life? What major changes are you going through? Resolve those and you'll most likely resolve your sleeping problems, too.

100 *Get Lash Extensions*

If there is one instant beautifier worth spending money on, it's lash extensions. They have revolutionized my eyes—and hey, my life! They are expensive but worth every cent. You'll be transformed from a normal pretty girl to a Hollywood goddess in just a few flutters of your eyelids.

Let me explain the process: you go to a beautician and lie down on a massage bed for two hours while individual fake lashes are glued to your individual real lashes. Don't think this is anything like the clumpy old-school falsies you bought from the drugstore in high school. These look natural. In fact, once they have been applied, you'll look like yourself, just a little bit better—and the best bit is that people won't be able to guess why. They are natural looking, so you won't look like a drag queen during the day, and they last for around two months.

I discovered these tiny black strips of heaven a year ago. It was in the heat of summer and I was feeling a bit dowdy. But I knew I had to get out there. I booked a trip to Spain and got a new summer wardrobe, and then a fabulously in-the-know beauty writer told me about extensions. She gave me a wink, and I couldn't believe it. I had always thought she was just blessed with Bambi-style lashes, but no—and she was sharing her secret with me.

I went off to Spain a new woman. Flirting became easier when I knew my darker eyes stayed seductive all night—I didn't need to worry about my mascara or eye shadow sliding down my face after a few glasses of sangria and a quick flamenco dance at the local nightclub.

And they withstood sea, sun, and sand. I went skinny-dipping in the ocean at midnight and they stayed put. I played volleyball in a swimming pool and not one dropped off. In fact, when daytime vacation photos were normally something to be avoided at all costs, my new lashes added an element to my whole face that made me look fab even without any makeup on!

They cost quite a bit (two hundred dollars is about average) and they need to be reapplied every eight weeks, but makeup becomes redundant, your confidence is given a boost, and your eyes will look amazing. What's not to love?

DON'T JUST TAKE IT FROM ME . . .

"I have everyone from my colleagues to my mom addicted to lash extensions now. It is slightly awkward having them applied and your eyes can sting a little after, but the effect makes it worth it. After all, beauty is pain."

Holly, 35, beauty editor, New York City

"When I was planning my wedding, I was very particular about looking sophisticated and elegant. Vivien Leigh was my inspiration, and I noticed she had spectacular lashes. Not being naturally blessed, I went to my local beauty salon to try the latest gimmick—extensions. The difference was subtle yet amazing, and they stayed on for the whole honeymoon. The one problem is that I'm now addicted. I think my husband has forgotten that I don't naturally look like this, so I'm having to pay quite a bit to keep up the illusion!"

Claire, 33, bank manager, London

IF YOU CAN'T GET LASH EXTENSIONS . . .

Invest in a super-duper, fortifying, extending, and tripling mascara. There are a plethora of them on the market now, and they can exaggerate your look with two coats. Black is the most dramatic, but brown or gray looks more natural on paler people. The downsides to mascara are occasional clumping and flaking and having to remove it every night, but it is undoubtedly cheaper than getting extensions and available in every pharmacy in the country.

101 Have a Pro Do Your Makeup

We all want to look gorgeous, but sometimes we get stuck in a rut. I know I do. I recently saw a friend I hadn't seen since college and he remarked on how I hadn't changed a bit. At first I thought this was marvelous (I pride myself on my nearly wrinkle-free forehead), but then I got to thinking: I really do have the same haircut, style, and makeup routine as I did all those years ago when I was nineteen. Had I not learned anything about becoming a sophisticated thirty-something? Did my increase in pay not show up as an increase in my glamour stakes?

The easiest thing to remedy was my makeup. A good makeover is easily available at any good department store or shopping mall, and the changes recommended won't break the bank.

Why should you hire a professional? Well, her or his job is to look at faces. She spends all day observing shapes, faults, things worth highlighting, and how to do so. She also know the tricks of colors and camouflage.

As much as we may think we look at ourselves objectively, we don't. We feel ugly when we're hungover, sultry if we've just had sex, pale when we've had a late night. Asking a pro to look at your face and analyze your makeup bag and routine will allow you the chance to break bad habits and start fresh—with a collection of products, tools, and ideas that suit the new you and that won't be difficult to maintain.

DON'T JUST TAKE IT FROM ME . . .

"I have a tragically square face, and, short of chiseling away at my jawbone with a knife, I thought there was nothing I could do about it. A makeup artist friend of a friend offered to help me out and gave me great tips on how to shade areas of my face I didn't like in order to take the emphasis off them. I feel so much more confident now."

Morgan, 24, receptionist, New York City

"I have always found inspiration in magazines and from celebrities' looks on the red carpet, but I never knew how to implement it. One session with a makeup pro taught me the stars' tricks of the trade—and how to wear makeup without looking as though I am trying too hard. I want to look like an improved version of myself and I now know how to achieve that."

Tracy, 32, computer technician, Dallas

IF YOU CAN'T HAVE A PRO DO YOUR MAKEUP . . .

Consume the beauty pages of your favorite magazines. Cut out and keep any ideas, styles, tips, and products you think would suit you, your face shape, and your lifestyle.

ABOUT THE AUTHOR

Sarah Ivens is an editor at large for *OK!* magazine's U.S. edition, the eighth-biggest retail magazine in America with a weekly circulation of one million. She appears regularly on *Good Morning America,* the *Today* show, *Entertainment Tonight, The Insider, E! News,* and *Extra* and was recently a featured guest judge on the WE tv's top-rated show, *American Princess* and was a judge on Miss America 2008. Her writing has been featured in *Brides, Cosmopolitan, Glamour, Marie Claire,* and *Men's Health.*

A born and bred Londoner who now lives in Brooklyn, New York, Ivens is a best-selling author in her native England, with seven books published in the UK and internationally. *No Regrets* is her American debut.